CUMBRIA COUNTY LIBRARY
3 8003 03345 3879
WITHDRAWN

D0507740

SPIRITUAL COMPASS

The three qualities of life

SPIRITUAL COMPASS

The three qualities of life

SATISH KUMAR

with illustrations by Truda Lane

Green Books

Published in 2007
by Green Books Ltd
Foxhole, Dartington
Totnes, Devon TQ9 6EB
edit@greenbooks.co.uk
www.greenbooks.co.uk

The quotation by Einstein on page 62 is from
Ideas and Opinions, edited by Carl Seelig, Bonzana Books, 1954.

The quotation by Thich Nhat Hanh on page 63 is from
Entering the Stream, Shambhala, 1993.

Cover design by Rick Lawrence
samskara@onetel.com

Text printed by TJ International Ltd, Padstow, UK
on Five Seasons 100% recycled paper

ISBN 978 1 903998 89 2

CONTENTS

ACKNOWLEDGEMENTS

I am indebted to my friend Rukmini Sekhar who suggested that I should write a book about the three qualities of life. The first and second chapters of this book were published by the Viveka Foundation in India in 2006.

I would like to thank Claire and Roger Ash Wheeler for their kind and generous hospitality in letting me use the tranquil and beautiful boathouse on the River Dart where I was able to write this book undisturbed.

I would like to express my gratitude to June, my wife, for her help and inspiration, without which this book would not have been written. I am grateful to Maya, my daughter, who worked with me on the first chapter, editing, revising and expanding it. I would like to thank Juliette Collins, who gave much of her time and attention during the final stages of preparing the book, and John Lane for his critical reading of the text and many helpful comments.

A SPIRITUAL COMPASS

When we are on a journey we need a compass; even when we are at sea, surrounded by great waves, a compass can help us to find our direction. In the same way we need a spiritual compass to find our direction in life.

A spiritual compass can help us to navigate our path through confusion and crises, through the suffocating allure of materialism, and through delusion and despair.

The ancient Indian tradition of Ayurveda offers us such a compass: a compass of three qualities. This compass can help us to find the way of wholesome living.

ALLĀH

PREFACE

Modern science recognises that nature is a play of the forces of creativity, transformation and inertia. When these forces are in balance, nature—including human nature—is in balance, and our lives express themselves in physical, emotional and spiritual wellbeing. The ancient Vedic tradition of wisdom defined these three forces in a similar way: they are named *sattva, rajas* and *tamas,* and are the governing principles in all of nature.

Sattva relates to creativity; *rajas* to energy; and *tamas* to inertia. At the present time humanity suffers from an excess of *rajas.* When *rajas* is out of balance and in excess, the outcome is an inflammation in all areas of life. Inflammation in the body is linked to an increased incidence of heart attacks, auto-immune diseases, cancer, and many other illnesses. Inflammation in the mind and emotions produces anger, hostility, resentment and grievances. Inflammation in society produces war and terrorism. Today's illness is the symptom of too much *rajas,* leading to the conditions of *tamas.*

In this book Satish Kumar offers a holistic approach to humanity's problems by showing how a *sattvic* lifestyle can allow us to heal ourselves and contribute to the healing of humanity and the world.

Those who wish to restore the broken balance in their lives will greatly benefit from the wisdom expounded in this book.

Deepak Chopra

FOREWORD

We are facing an unprecedented global crisis. That much is clear. Not a day goes by without the news media reminding us of climate change, endangered species, economic instability, pollution, poverty, famine, terrorism or war. Such problems are not separate, independent, issues. The Club of Rome, in its seminal report *The Limits to Growth,* called them a "global problematique", a complex intertwined set of problems. Yet, we usually treat them in isolation. We seek to control scarce resources, cap carbon emissions, fine the polluters, shore up failing banks, destroy terrorists and punish drug users. We seldom look into the root causes of our various problems.

We would not do this with our own bodies. If we visited a doctor because of a bad stomach pain, and all the doctor did was give us a painkiller, we would not think him or her a very good doctor. A good doctor would inquire deeper, to the cause of the pain. Is it something we've eaten? Is there an infection? Or is it, perhaps, due to stress? If the root cause is left untreated, then the symptoms will almost surely return. When it comes to treating our global malaise, however, we don't often consider the underlying issues. We focus on dealing with the many symptoms, then wonder why the problems haven't gone away.

When we inquire into what lies behind the global problematique, we find, time and again, human factors—human decisions, human thinking and human values. The crisis we are facing is, in essence, a crisis of consciousness—a crisis of perception and values. It is becoming increasingly clear that the dominating materialist values of efficiency and economy need to be balanced by the equally important values of care, compassion and respect.

Such values are not foreign to any of us, and can be found in all cultures. However, Western society's over-emphasis of life's material side has so filled our minds with wants, worries, schemes and regrets, these qualities seldom surface. The world's spiritual traditions, on the other hand, have safeguarded and encouraged such values. They have repeatedly reminded us of the truths we all know inside, but which are so easily overlooked in our struggle to make it in the world.

In the Vedas of ancient India it is held that everything is permeated by three fundamental qualities—the three *gunas—sattva, rajas* and *tamas. Sattva* means true, natural, nourishing; *rajas* is associated with change, achievement, excitement; *tamas* is connected with weight, control, inertia. Nothing is without these three qualities; what is important is which one dominates.

The notion of the three *gunas* may be new to many of us, but they have informed Indian culture for thousands of years. In recent times, Mahatma Gandhi exemplified a life dominated by *sattvic* values, revealing the quiet power of humility and non-violence. *Spiritual Compass* is a call for us all to live more *sattvic* lives. This does not mean giving up our worldly lives; it is an encouragement to live a more balanced life, one that is in harmony with our surroundings, neither taking too much, nor destroying unnecessarily.

Few people are better qualified to write this book than Satish Kumar. His own upbringing as a Jain monk in India has given him a deep personal intimacy with these principles. Living the last thirty years in the West has shown him both the need and practicality of applying these principles to daily affairs. Most importantly, his own life is an admirable example of simplicity, compassion and care. And this shines through on every page of this delightful, yet profound, little book.

Peter Russell

AN INVITATION

Dear Reader

I would like to invite you to learn three new words in order to enjoy this book. These ancient words are from the Sanskrit language, and have been commonly used in India for millennia; they serve as a useful aid to good living.

The first word is *sattvic,* which I translate as elegant and simple. Basically this word is used to remind people to follow the way which rings true to them at the deepest level, which is natural and real. Therefore it is to be embraced.

The second word is *rajasic* which can be translated as extravagant and excessive. This word is used to warn people of the pitfalls of the glittering and the glamorous. Even though the rajasic way of living may be tempting, because of its complicated nature it will tend to bring disappointment and discontentment; therefore it is generally to be avoided.

The third word is *tamasic,* which I have defined as dark and depressing. This word is used as an alarm bell to alert people about danger ahead. Tamasic acts may appeal to people as daring and exciting, but the experience of wise people in the past has shown again and again that tamasic is destructive, disempowering and confusing; therefore it is strenuously to be avoided.

I will be using these three words throughout the book and explaining their multi-layered meaning, and their relevance in the context of environment, development, food, farming, politics, power and much more. I will be making the obvious case for a sattvic life, and showing that elegant simplicity is a spiritual imperative.

These three qualities of life are as much external attributes as they are an internal state of being. Inner intentions and motivations are as important as outer actions. So we are not to judge people only by their external appearances.

Ultimately there is the state of transcendence. At that secret centre of our being there are no compartments, no labels and no categories; no sattvic, no rajasic and no tamasic. We rise above all dualities and divisions, and live in perfect harmony with ourselves and the world around us. That is the state of unselfconscious existence. At that stage one is fully self-realised.

So, to live a good life, it helps to be aware of the sattvic, rajasic and tamasic qualities in everything. Firstly we need to develop a sense of proportion, and the right mix of sattvic, rajasic and tamasic; secondly, to make the right and appropriate choices; and thirdly, to rise above them. Then joy is ours, and we will be able to live happier lives.

THE THREE QUALITIES OF LIFE ACCORDING TO THE BHAGAVAD GITA

Three Kinds of Food

Foods which promote vitality, health and joy, which are soft, sweet and nourishing are sattvic.

Foods which produce pain, grief and disease, which are bitter, sour, pungent and harsh are rajasic.

Foods which produce dullness, heaviness and lethargy, which are tasteless, stale and intoxicating are tamasic.

Three Kinds of Service

Service which is offered in accordance with the natural laws, expecting no reward in return is sattvic.

Service which is offered for display, for gain and reward is rajasic.

Service which is offered without faith and with an empty heart is tamasic.

Three Kinds of Practice

Pure, upright and non-violent acts, non-offensive, truthful, pleasant and beneficial speech, and gentle, serene and restrained thoughts are sattvic.

Practice which is performed for gain and honour is rajasic.

Practice which is obstinate and causes injury to oneself and to others is tamasic.

Three Kinds of Gifts

A gift which is made with pure motives, without expecting anything in return, given at an appropriate place and time is sattvic.

A gift which is made with the expectation of something in return is rajasic.

A gift which is made with contempt and which demeans the receiver is tamasic.

Three Kinds of Understanding

Understanding which sees unity in diversity, wholeness, relatedness and creates synthesis is sattvic.

Understanding which is based in disunity and causes separation is rajasic.

Understanding which focuses on a part and sees it as if it was the whole is tamasic.

Three Kinds of Action

Action which is performed without attachment, without desire for reward and with love is sattvic.

Action which is performed under stress and for the purpose of gratification is rajasic.

Action which is performed in ignorance, without regard for consequences and which brings injury is tamasic.

Three Kinds of Person

The person who has no ego and who is unperturbed by either success or failure is sattvic.

The person who is swayed by passion, who eagerly seeks results and who is greedy is rajasic.

The person who is unbalanced, vulgar, deceitful, malicious and despondent is tamasic.

Three Kinds of Thinking

The thinking which knows the difference between right and wrong action, what is to be feared and not to be feared, and what brings freedom and what brings bondage is sattvic.

The thinking which is confused between right and wrong, courage and cowardice is rajasic.

The thinking which conceives right as wrong and wrong as right is tamasic.

Three Kinds of Determination

Determination which maintains balance and harmony between thinking, breathing and sensing is sattvic.

Determination which seeks to fulfil the desire for wealth and power is rajasic.

Determination which brings depression, arrogance, grief and fear is tamasic.

Three Kinds of Happiness

Happiness which is a result of a clear understanding of the self and the world is sattvic.

Happiness which arises from the gratification of the senses, which seems like nectar at first but is like poison at the end is rajasic.

Happiness which comes from delusion and which is derived from sloth and negligence is tamasic.

Chapter One

THE THREE QUALITIES OF LIFE

A Way Out of Anguish

WE LIVE IN an age of anguish.

Political anguish makes civilised nations behave like barbarians, and superpowers live in fear. Rulers know not the art of ruling. Politicians in high office have little skill in solving problems. Ongoing conflicts in Palestine, Israel, Iraq, Afghanistan, Kashmir and Sri Lanka, to name but a few, show both the intractable nature of the problems and the incapacity of those in power to resolve them. Fighting and killing are the principal means used to resolve discord and disharmony. People seem unable to find solutions which are just, fair and satisfactory to all.

Social anguish manifests itself when society allows people to die of starvation in the midst of plenty. Even though the struggle against debt and deprivation has been going on for decades, with governments, UN agencies and aid organisations pouring money and materials into deprived areas, yet an end to hunger remains a distant dream. It is a cliché, but nevertheless true, that the rich keep getting richer and the poor get poorer.

Farmers and food growers cannot make ends meet. Too many of them end up committing suicide. Rural people are losing their livelihoods and rushing to the cities, where they work in slavish conditions or are compelled to beg on the streets and live in slums.

Ecological anguish is evident as we destroy the environment which sustains our lives. We have lost a sense of balance between the rights of humans and the rights of nature. Much of what is considered to be economic, scientific and technological progress is causing severe stress to the soil, air and water. Despite constant warnings from scientists, neither governmental nor industrial leaders seem to know how to inspire and persuade people to change their ways so as to halt the pattern of ecological destruction and lead the world towards a sustainable future.

Our spiritual anguish is equally poignant. Established religions often provide no satisfactory sustenance to our souls. Traditional communities and extended families no longer exist in modern urban societies to provide the psychological and emotional support which is essential to our wellbeing. Rituals and ceremonies, which used to create a space for spiritual enrichment, have all but disappeared. Religious and cultural festivals which brought joy and a sense of celebration have too often been commercialised and turned into occasions for shopping and consuming.

The arts are more and more commercialised. They may make us celebrities and boost our egos, if we are lucky. They may bring us money, if we are successful, but spiritually they remain ineffectual.

What can we do? Where can we go? How can we feed the imagination? Where can we find inspiration? When can we nourish the soul? The culture of our time seems to have no answers.

PERHAPS ANCIENT WISDOM could offer us some clues to understanding who we are, what our nature is, and how we can create a pattern of living which is harmonious, integrated and balanced.

In Indian thought, there is a way to perceive the world as being made up of three qualities called *gunas*. When we see ourselves and understand our condition using the three qualities as a compass, they can tell us who we are and where we are. They can orient us towards the direction in which we wish to go. They can help us to recover the art of living and lead us out of our anguish towards a peaceful, joyful and contented existence. The three qualities can be interpreted in the modern context. They can throw light on the predicament of our anguished humanity. They can convey some ancient wisdom to the modern world. Through them we can relate to our everyday life—our food, clothing, agriculture, architecture, power structures, communication methods and problem-solving.

The Meaning of the Three Qualities

Sattvic is buoyant and shining
Rajasic is stimulating and moving
Tamasic is heavy and dominating
They illuminate the human path like a lamp
Ishvarakrishna, Samkhyakarika verses 12 & 13, 3rd to 5th century

The concept of the three qualities was developed as part of the philosophy and practice of Ayurveda, the traditional Indian health system dating back nearly 5,000 years. Ayurveda is a way of cultivating and maintaining our personal and social health as well as the health of the planet, and it is still practised widely in India.

In Ayurveda, physical wellbeing is dependent on two interconnected aspects: on the one hand, a healthy mind is the prerequisite of a healthy body, and on the other, without a healthy society and a healthy environment, personal health will remain a distant dream.

All objects, all thoughts, all actions and all relationships have one or the other of these three qualities or tendencies (or a combination of two, or all three of them), but one particular quality is always predominant.

In Sanskrit, these three qualities are called *sattvic, rajasic* and *tamasic.*

Sattvic means true, natural, uncorrupted, original, simple, sincere, good, delightful, honest, undiluted, refreshing, lucid, luminous and spiritual.

Rajasic means regal, royal, shining, glorious, glamorous, glittering, sophisticated, seductive, splendid, strong, extravagant and exciting. The word for 'kingdom' in most Indian languages is 'raj'. So *rajas* is connected with political power and prestige.

Tamasic means dark, dulling, depressing, sinister, ugly, fearful, dictatorial, diseased, heavy and harmful.

Sattvic focuses on the purity of means.

Rajasic is concerned with achieving the ends.

For tamasic, the end justifies the means.

Kindness is sattvic, anger is rajasic, and revenge is tamasic.

Sattvic seeks fulfilment, rajasic, success, and tamasic, control.

These three qualities provide a map of three personality types. A sattvic mind appreciates and celebrates the intrinsic goodness of the natural world. Up or down, light or dark, flower or thorn, nature embodies complementary opposites. Maintaining a balance and harmony of opposites is the way of the sattvic: a recognition and understanding of things as they are, without judgement or desire to alter, flowing with the flow, going with the grain and remaining equanimous, is the sphere of the sattvic.

The rajasic mind leans towards the improvement of things. It believes that the raw and rugged realities of the natural world can be reformed and changed or even engineered to make them better suited to human purpose. In the rajasic mind, cultivated flowers are better than wild flowers; the splendour of exotic flowers in a magnificent vase is better than flowers in a field.

In the tamasic mind, the original or the natural is no good at all. The tamasic mind sees nature as red in tooth and claw. So tamasic tries to move away from nature as far as it can. Natural flowers are impermanent—they have to be renewed, they even die and have to be cleared away, so tamasic is attracted to plastic flowers. Tamasic divorces the idea of beauty from its source, and is attracted to an alien and artificial version of reality.

Life is like a river. The normal, steady and slow flow is sattvic. Only through its flow does the river keep its freshness. Then occasionally the river flows over a cliff in a dramatic way and forms a great waterfall—that is a rajasic event. In some places, the water is blocked and becomes stagnant, impure and polluted. That state is tamasic.

The sattvic way of life is available to everyone. It is authentic, ordinary; it is everyday life, and does not require a great deal of money and resources. It is simple, sincere, unassuming and sublime. The sattvic life derives its sustenance from the sun, moon and stars, from oceans, mountain peaks and forests. This sattvic quality is related to culture, community and creativity. It is spiritual and subtle; it is easy and self-organising. It does not make heavy demands on natural resources. It has only a small footprint on the Earth. It is sustaining and sustainable. It is fulfilling and healing.

People with a sattvic bent of mind get on with the business of life in small steps, trusting the process of the universe and believing that things will work out. People living a sattvic life may not consider themselves sattvic or claim to be sattvic. Cooking fresh food at home, taking care of children and guests, growing vegetables and fruit in their gardens, maintaining small farms, workshops and crafts, mending and repairing—all fall within the sattvic way of life.

To quote from an ancient Indian text, *Shilpa Shastra*, “A sattvic person is a good human being, generous in spirit, not given to anger, holy, learned, self-controlled, devout, charitable and taking delight in the care of the self and the care of the Earth.”

This idea of sattva is comparable to the *Wabi-Sabi* of Japan, the Zen of Buddhism, the Tao of China, the Sufi way of Islam and the ways of the Shakers and the Amish. Sattva seeks synthesis, integrity and diversity. It is about *being* rather than *having*, it values stillness and silence, it celebrates less rather than more, it is appreciative and affirmative.

The sattvic person embodies firmness, courage, self-command, good sense, magnanimity and wisdom. The sattvic mind leads to inner and outer freedom, freedom for oneself as well as for others.

There is a Sanskrit verse which Mahatma Gandhi recited every day during morning and evening prayers, which encapsulates the sattvic spirit: “I do not desire kingdom, heaven, paradise or even nirvana. I only desire the end of suffering of all beings upon this Earth.” In this prayer, Gandhi did not seek nirvana for himself; he only desired the end of suffering for others; he was in a space of total generosity. As a consequence, he was in a state of nirvana even though he did not desire it. This is the quality of a sattvic person.

A rajasic person wanders from temple to temple, from book to book, from one spiritual technique to another, resorts to drugs, psychotherapy or some other method, searching, seeking and longing for nirvana or enlightenment for him- or herself. Yet such self-seeking is no help in attaining nirvana. Sattva is a state of effortless being; rajas is a state of active seeking. Sattva finds miracles in the ordinary, magic in every moment; every day is a fine day, every breath is a breath of the universe, every river a sacred river and every mountain a holy mountain. Tamas shows up a destructive mind. It seeks pleasure by inflicting suffering on others. It attacks to defend itself. It destroys the interests of others to serve self-interest.

The rajasic way of life is the way of the elite. It is slick and analytical. It impresses and makes an impact; it celebrates speed, the grand and the extravagant. It likes big projects, big dams, big buildings, big power stations, big bridges, big stadiums and big shows. It concentrates on achievement, on outcome and on success. It admires celebrities, the prestigious and the powerful. It likes display, decoration and extravaganzas. Rajas does not mind waste. It often pays lip service to fairness and justice but then moves on to serve its own interest. It loves technological solutions and elaborate plans to conquer space. Rajasic rulers claim to favour freedom but in practice they impose their rule through domination and control. They believe that the rajasic path is superior and that it will be possible for everyone to be on it. The rajasic way of life is dependent on excessive use of natural resources, and values nature only in terms of her usefulness to humans. It believes in scientific progress, technological development and economic growth. Rajas relishes power, money and the military. It hungers for comfort and convenience.

The tamasic tendency relates to the forces of darkness. It is dictatorial, cunning, fearful and secretive. It produces depression, dullness, apathy and inertia. It is associated with casinos, the underworld, the black market, brothels, crime, drugs, prisons and torture. The tamasic way leads to factory farming, to huge slaughterhouses, to genetic engineering and to large-scale mining. Sometimes what starts off as sattva grows into rajas and then degenerates into tamas. For example, fishing on a small scale as a source of sattvic livelihood to feed a community can grow into a rajasic business where it still maintains a certain social responsibility and some environmental concern, but when the business grows into a fleet of factory ships, spreading miles of nets, depleting fish stocks, exporting fish around the world and destroying the small-boat fishing culture along with its dependent communities, then rajasic has turned into tamasic.

When an economy provides a livelihood for individuals and families, it is a sattvic economy. When the economy grows large, motivated by profit, but still operates within the parameters of social responsibility, then it is a rajasic economy. But when humans and the Earth are used to *serve* the economy; then it turns into a tamasic economy. Most multinational corporations operate in a tamasic way, in what Joel Bakan calls "the pathological pursuit of profit and power".

Political power is always rajasic, but it can turn easily from rajasic to tamasic. The rulers managing, maintaining and organising the affairs of their own country are rajasic, but when they colonise, build empires, wage wars of conquest and destroy other cultures, then rajasic politics becomes tamasic; the queen in her kingdom and the president of a republic ruling with the consent of their peoples, are rajasic; but when the kingdom becomes an empire or a democracy turns into a dictatorship, then it is tamasic.

Likewise, when soldiers defend the weak of their own country against invasions while acting with appropriate force, then they are within the rajasic realm. But when armies bomb other countries, indiscriminately killing civilians calling it 'collateral damage', using disproportionate force backed by nuclear weapons, then that army has become a tamasic force. Abuse, violation of human rights and torture are intrinsically part of tamasic action.

Thus the sattvic tendency is always towards minimum impact. The sattvic approach to economics and politics is a quest for simple, long-lasting benefits and non-violent means.

The sattvic way seeks wholeness and harmony.

The Three Qualities in Communication: Dialogue, Diplomacy and Monologue

THE SATTVIC WAY is the way of dialogue. In dialogue, we are engaged in mutual exploration and understanding. There is no fixed position, no dogma, no desire to convert; rather, there is a desire to reach a stage which is respectful to all sides and honours the intrinsic qualities of every position, making dialogue a conversation among equals. We can be in dialogue with people, with nature and with ourselves. Dialogue happens with open minds and open hearts. It reaches compromise in the ambit of the true meaning of the word: 'promising together'.

In dialogue, change comes about from within and emerges out of shared understanding, instead of change being imposed from without. In dialogue, unexpected insights emerge, things unfold, relationships deepen, ideas multiply, imagination is enhanced and everyone is engaged in a process of discovery. Everyone participates, all sides are active.

The rajasic way is the way of diplomacy. Diplomacy can conceal a fixed position and self-interest, but outwardly show patience, politeness and peaceable intent. It tries to find a way to convince, to win over through argument, bargaining and even bribery. It tries to avoid confrontation or a breakdown in communication. It is the way of making deals, business contracts and political treaties. In diplomacy, razzmatazz is added—receptions are held, champagne flows, the ego is massaged, everyone is made to feel important and the red carpet is rolled out. This is the realm of rajas.

The tamasic way is the way of monologue. Monologue has blind faith in its own rightness. It starts from the position of 'I am right, you are wrong. You change, or else.' Monologue threatens, cajoles, calls names, denigrates, imposes and resorts to brute force. It leads to monopoly and monoculture. Tamas is trapped in monologue. It wants its own way, regardless. It embraces violence and is driven by anger, pride, greed, illusion and lust. Its methods are heavy-handed. It justifies errors and never recognises them, even when everyone can see that things have gone wrong; a tamasic person finds it hard to say sorry.

The tamasic approach shows a fear of losing from the outset, while the sattvic approach is based in trust: trust in oneself, trust in the other and trust in the process of communication.

The Three Qualities of Time: Present, Future and Past

TIME, TOO, CAN BE understood in terms of these three qualities. Living in the here and now, acting spontaneously and unselfconsciously, responding to a situation as it is and seeing the present moment as a beautiful moment is sattvic. In sattvic time there is no judgement, no gloss, no interpretation, for these belong either to the past or to the future; they are part of reflecting on what has already happened or planning what is to come. Living in the present moment, being satisfied with what is now, and feeling a sense of gratitude for all the gifts of the moment, is sattvic.

Here is a story:

A fisherman was lying in the sun on a beach, dozing. He had finished his fishing for the day; he had had his lunch, and now it was time for his rest.

A businessman noticed him lying down lazily, and asked, "Why are you not at work today?"

"I have finished my work. I went out in my little boat this morning, caught some fish, sold some, cooked and ate some; now it is time to rest, time for my siesta," said the fisherman.

"But you could catch some more fish, couldn't you?" asked the businessman.

"Why should I do that?" asked the fisherman in surprise.

"Then you could have some more money, buy a bigger boat with an engine which would carry much larger nets and catch even more fish," replied the businessman.

"Why?" asked the fisherman.

"Well, then you can have a fleet of boats, set up a company, and when it's successful, you can sell it and make lots of money," said the businessman.

"Then what?" The fisherman was at a loss.

"Then you can retire and lie on the beach without any worries, forever," insisted the businessman.

"But I am doing exactly that now. I am having my siesta. I have no worries about the future. I am happy, very happy. I have enough and enough is enough for me. I am blessed with the sea and the sunshine and plenty of time to enjoy life. Why would I go to all that trouble?"

The businessman, at first speechless, soon went away smiling.

The fisherman led a sattvic life—a life lived in the here and now. He was at peace.

Dwelling on the future is rajasic. Our minds become involved in exciting projects: "Let's do this, let's live there, let's keep it for a rainy day, let's have more, newer and better." All this planning and projecting is rajasic. We harbour many grand designs, blind to what is in front of us in the present moment.

Here is another story:

A young man called Sheikh Chili was standing in a marketplace. A merchant named Govinda asked him to carry a clay pot full of sesame oil to his house on the other side of town.

"I will pay you ten rupees," said Govinda.

"Fifteen rupees, sir," bargained Sheikh Chili.

"Okay, fifteen rupees, then," said the merchant.

Govinda helped Sheikh Chili to lift the clay pot and balance it on a cloth ring on top of his head. Sheikh Chili followed the merchant cheerfully and started to dream about his future....

"With fifteen rupees I will buy a hen and a rooster. The hen will produce eggs and I will have many chickens. I will sell the chickens and buy a nanny goat and a billy goat and they will produce many kids. I will sell the kids and get a lot of money and then I'll buy a cow and a calf. Eventually, I'll buy a house and then I'll be able to get married and with my wife's dowry I will have plenty of money. I will have children and they will call me for delicious dinners cooked by their mother…"

He was planning his future, and in absolute delight he opened both his arms wide, saying to his imaginary children, "Yes, yes, I'm coming; I'm coming for my dinner!" He forgot all about the oil pot on his head which fell clattering to the ground and broke to smithereens. Not only did the oil flow away into a nearby gutter, but the merchant angrily demanded that he pay for it and the oil. Sheikh Chili was in tears and in debt.

This is rajasic, living in the future. Living in the past is tamasic: "Why did you do that? Why didn't I do that? We shouldn't have done that!" We complain and moan. But the past is the past, it has come and gone, we cannot alter it. Living in the past is dull and depressing, diminishes our ability to be whole and deflects our attention from living fully in the present. The following story illustrates this:

Two monks, Ananda and Ashoka, came to a rapidly flowing river and were preparing to cross it. A young woman was standing on the bank also wanting to cross.

"Hey, monks—I am frightened to cross the river by myself but I must get to the other shore. Can you carry me, please? I am very light," she said.

The monks looked at her and hesitated. Then, after a few moments, Ananda went to her and said, "All right, get on my back."

He carried the woman across, reached the other shore and left her there.

The two monks continued their journey. But Ashoka kept thinking, "We are celibates. Ananda should never have come into such close contact with a woman. Her breasts were pressing against his body. She was holding him tight. And Ananda was holding the woman's thighs. This is wrong, wrong, wrong. This is against the rules." Ashoka became obsessed with these thoughts. He lost his peace of mind and was going through agony and agitation. Time passed and he kept brooding on these thoughts. After an hour or so, he could hold his tongue no longer. He lashed out at Ananda: "Ananda, what have you done, you have broken our vows of celibacy! You carried that woman on your back; that was wrong. You must confess to our teacher this evening."

"Ashoka, I left the woman at the river bank a long time ago," Ananda replied, "but you seem to be still carrying her in your head!"

Ananda was living in the present, a sattvic state while Ashoka was living in the past, a tamasic state.

Wise philosophers advise us to live in the present as much as we can, say 80 per cent of the time. Then we should negotiate our way towards the future; say 15 per cent of our time. Of course, we have to recognise that a bit of living in the past is inevitable, but we should keep it to the minimum and not allow it to overwhelm us. Five per cent of our time spent dealing with the past is more than enough.

The Three Qualities of Food: Sweet, Spicy and Stale

FOOD, TOO, IS SATTVIC, rajasic or tamasic. What can be easily digested is sattvic. Fruit ripened by the sun, requiring no effort of cooking and little effort in digesting is the most sattvic. There are fruitarians who eat fruits of the season and nothing else. Raw vegetables, such as salads and sprouting seeds, which require no cooking and are easy to digest, fall into the sattvic category. Beans, peas, pulses, potatoes, whole grains and small portions of sweets and puddings are all sattvic. The sattvic way of eating is slow and moderate. We should eat slightly less than our capacity so that when we have completed our meal we still feel light. Sattvic food is refreshing, tasty, naturally sweet, and when necessary, cooked lightly.

Food is shared with whoever is present—family, friends, guests or even strangers who drop in. A portion is offered to birds, animals and insects as co-custodians of the food we eat.

Sattvic food is grown and consumed locally. The culture of sattvic food implies that all of us participate in the growing, preparing or cooking of it in whatever way we can. Sattvic food is a gift of nature and not a commodity to buy and sell. Such food is available in abundance, there is no scarcity, it grows everywhere and is available to everyone, to all living beings—humans and other than humans. Sattvic discourages wastefulness; everything that comes from the land is returned to the land. No fertilisers, no chemicals, no pesticides, no herbicides, no demand on the land to give more than it can naturally give. And the food is received from the land with a sense of gratitude. Sattvic agriculture is always organic and natural.

What is not eaten is composted, and so is what is eaten, through the composting of urine and excrement. The land does not discriminate between bird droppings, animal dung and human excrement. Land and natural processes have a way of digesting and transforming everything into nutrients. Sattva implies a zero-waste existence. For a sattvic practitioner of life, nature shows the way of right living. Since there is no waste in nature, the sattvic way of human life too has no waste.

Humans, in sattva philosophy, are considered to be a *part* of nature, not *apart* from nature—there is no separation and no dualism between nature and humans, or between the natural way and the sattvic way. The natural way is the sattvic way and the sattvic way is the natural way.

Sattvic food is sacred food. In the sattvic worldview, the land is sacred, seeds are sacred, cultivating and the cultivator are sacred, cooking is sacred, eating is sacred, washing up is sacred. In rural India, farmers practising the traditional form of farming never sell seed. If a farmer is in need of seed, then it is freely shared.

Rajasic food is exciting and stimulating. Onions, garlic and chili as well as spicy, salty, fatty and fried foods are rajasic. Rajasic cuisine is elaborate. It may be prepared by celebrity chefs to be talked about and presented at parties and banquets. It is more about looks and presentation than nutrition. It is fashionable food. It is food imported from afar without heed to season or food miles. Rajasic food is aristocratic—those who eat it do not participate in cooking or growing it, and those who grow and cook are seen to be inferior to those who eat it. There is much waste, and the food itself is considered less important than the one who eats it. Rajasic food is a mere commodity to be bought and sold.

Rajasic farmers think of themselves as 'owners' of the land. Other humans and wild creatures are considered to be trespassers—humans are fenced out and wildlife, which is deemed to be interfering with the crop, is turfed out. Land and nature are valued only in terms of their utility to the owners. There is no recognition of the intrinsic value of every form of life. Conservation, land management, agriculture and animal husbandry are undertaken primarily for the benefit of the owners.

Tamasic food is intoxicating, dulling, depressing and more difficult to digest. Alcohol, meat, preservatives, drugs and foods that are old or stale fall into the tamas category. Overeating, obesity and drunkenness are tamasic. Fast food, junk food, long-life, ready-made food and over-processed food, food which has no nutritional value, such as cola and other fizzy drinks, are full of tamas. The tamasic impulse wants to cut costs, control processes and find shortcuts to produce certain flavours. Food produced with excessive violence such as shrimp and salmon farming in cages, chickens in batteries, pigs in pens, calves in dark stalls, cows in confined spaces, and deer hunted by hounds, come into the tamasic category.

Whether food is tamasic is also determined to some extent by one's attitude to it. Hunters in traditional cultures take life only to meet their vital needs. In cold climates such as the Arctic, Siberia or Tibet, where vegetation is sparse and only available for a very limited period of the year, the hunting of animals to meet human needs is not tamasic. But when animals are made to suffer and when they are manipulated and their lives controlled to suit the taste of the tongue, then that is tamasic. How can one eat the meat of petrified and unhappy animals and not imbibe some of those negative qualities ourselves? When animals are kept alive under artificial conditions with drugs, hormones and antibiotics, and then are eaten by human beings, then there is no way to avoid adverse consequences on human health and the human psyche. Such external behaviour, which inflicts cruelty on animals and nature is bound to foster an internal cruelty within humans. Tamasic food leads to tamasic behaviour.

Industrialised agribusiness, which destroys biodiversity and produces mono-crops using heavy machinery, chemical fertilisers, pesticides and herbicides, is tamasic farming. Food is produced to make a profit rather than to feed people. Crops are burnt or thrown away to keep the market value high. Food mountains are maintained while people starve and die of hunger. This is tamas at its worst.

There are 300 million species on this Earth. All of them are fed and watered without the interference of the market. But in the tamasic system, land, forests and rivers are owned by a select few and large numbers of people are deprived of access to food and water. No other species suffers starvation; hunger is only a human phenomenon. Wise people have always urged society to avoid such tamasic ways of producing, distributing and managing food.

Tamas sees nature as inferior, inadequate, incomplete and imperfect. Tamasic people, in their arrogance, ignorance and greed engage in manipulations of natural systems, believing that they can improve nature for their benefit. The so-called 'green revolution', where hybrid seeds were developed with huge chemical inputs, irrigation and large-scale mechanised equipment, employed tamasic methods to produce food. The idea of the green revolution has continued in the growth of genetic manipulation, genetic engineering and terminator technologies, where seed production becomes the monopoly of a few big companies such as Monsanto, Cargill and Dupont, and where seeds lose their reproductive potency. This is human dictatorship over nature being touted as progress and development. In reality it is tamasic agriculture.

Communities practising the sattvic system of producing food—maintaining land, saving seed and celebrating the elegance of a simple life—are seen as backward and underdeveloped, and are subdued by the tamasic baton of aggressive force. But in reality people practising a sattvic relationship with food enjoy better health and vitality because they are treating food as food.

The Three Qualities of Buildings: Homes, Palaces and Prisons

A SATTVIC HOUSE IS a home: comfortable, pleasing, sufficient and serene. It sits easily in the landscape. Such a building is *of* the landscape rather than *on* it. It is in harmony with its surroundings. It is built not to impress but to accommodate. It makes frugal use of materials, and those materials are local, natural and organic. Cob, cloth, leather, straw, wood, stone, slate, thatch, earth and even glass used in moderation can be called sattvic materials. These structures, made by hand, are built to last, and the older they get the more they mature and charm. There is no contrived beauty in them, it is implicit and substantive. Sattvic dwellings gently unfold as they are built, and more is added as and when the need arises. They evolve according to climatic conditions, geography, culture and lifestyles. Tepees, yurts, igloos, huts, tents, cottages, farmhouses, barns, bungalows, longhouses, terraces, gypsy caravans, gatehouses and many other forms of dwellings which have developed over the centuries around the world, creating villages, market towns, neighbourhoods and city squares, are all sattvic forms. These buildings not only meet the physical needs of the inhabitants, they also meet their emotional, psychological and spiritual needs. When homes are built with love and care they generate an invisible quality of harmony, care, contentment and satisfaction. Sattvic homes are more than functional enclosures; they contain soul quality, they have spirit.

Rajasic buildings make a statement of importance. Palaces, pyramids, castles, cathedrals, domes, parliaments, town halls, guildhalls, concert halls, theatres, opera houses, stadiums, ocean liners and big yachts are rajasic buildings. They project power, authority, splendour and status. They are built of marble, quarried and faced stone; sometimes they are walled in, protected, fortified and guarded to keep the elite safe and the multitudes out.

Tamasic buildings are all utility and no beauty. Prisons, nuclear and other underground bunkers as well as military barracks are obvious examples of tamasic structures, but even the soulless structures of some modern hospitals, schools and shopping malls are equally tamasic. High-rise inner city towers and housing estates, where people are boxed together in a soulless environment with no space to breathe, no trees to shelter, no grass, no earth, no water, no flowers, are tamasic. Such edifices produce depression, crime and alienation.

Tamasic structures are built with cement, concrete, breezeblocks, steel, plastic, fibreglass, asbestos and other inorganic and unnatural materials which fail to please. People who live in them lose a sense of belonging and a sense of community. These buildings cause pollution, waste and disease. They are heavy on the environment—for example, the buildings in one square mile of Canary Wharf, London, with their systems and equipment, which first heat up and then have to cool, use as much electricity as the whole of Wales. Such profligate use of resources is tamasic. Buildings of this kind make no use of sunlight or fresh air. They are heated artificially, cooled artificially, lit artificially and ventilated artificially, using a great deal of fossil fuel and causing global warming and climate change. These systems are controlled by computers, and the people using these buildings can neither reduce nor increase cooling, heating, light or ventilation. Architecture of this nature, which imposes, dictates and controls human behaviour is purely tamasic because it lacks tranquillity, sincerity, authenticity and sustainability. There is no sense of human responsibility in such architecture.

Architecture which imposes itself on the lives of those who use the space is rajasic or tamasic, while sattvic buildings lend themselves to being lived in. They receive their inhabitants in a hospitable way, providing rest and peace from the bustle of the world, stimulating imagination and creativity.

The Three Qualities of Clothing: Cotton, Silk and Synthetic

CLOTH HAS THE SAME three qualities. The sattvic way of dressing and furnishing is comfortable, pleasing, adapted to the climate and made of local and natural materials. Cotton, linen, wool, jute, hemp, and other similar natural fibres are used to make sattvic cloth. Sattvic clothes are hand-made, hand-stitched, hand-spun, hand-woven, hand-embroidered, hand-painted and hand-dyed. They are beautiful, useful and durable at the same time. They are repaired, mended and altered; when worn out they are reused in quilts, patchwork, appliqué, rugs or just plain rags for cleaning.

Sattvic clothes are in sattvic colours—natural, unbleached and treated with organic natural vegetable dyes. These colours are gentle on the eye, earthy, soft, variable, and impermanent. The cloth is dyed and re-dyed.

Where I grew up, in Rajasthan, India, colours have meaning and are symbolic: brown is the colour of spirit; yellow is the colour of peace; white is the colour of purity; green is the colour of renewal; red is the colour of love.

Rajasic clothes are impressive, splendid, exuberant, attractive, and draw attention. Silk, satin, cashmere and pashmina are particularly rajasic materials. Rajasic cloth has gold and silver woven or embroidered on to it, sometimes even with pearls and precious stones. Ornaments and jewellery made of gold and diamonds are rajasic. Typically, rajasic clothes have designer labels; they are expensive and subject to short-lived fashions. Every year there are new clothes, with no concern for repairing, reusing, recycling and dyeing. Often clothes are made to be worn only on one occasion and then discarded

Rajasic colours are made permanent with the use of chemicals. Matching accessories accentuate the power and position of the wearer. A rajasic wardrobe is extensive and excessive; there is pride in 'possessing' rather than 'needing'. Rajasic dressing is 'power dressing'.

The legendary example is that of Imelda Marcos with her thousands of pairs of shoes.

Here is an interesting episode from the life of Mahatma Gandhi. When he was in England, he had an audience with the King. Subsequently, he was asked by a journalist, "How did you feel meeting the King in a loincloth, Mr Gandhi?"

"I was perfectly comfortable, since the King was wearing enough clothes for the both of us!" replied the Mahatma. The King was in rajasic clothing, while the Mahatma was in sattvic.

Tamasic clothing is frightening and sinister. Black leather trousers with studs, dark glasses, black leather jackets, heavy metal bracelets and necklaces, tough leather boots and helmets are typical. Vulgar, startling, flesh-revealing styles are also tamasic. These are clothes of seduction or domination, inducing fear or submission. Sometimes the cloth is artificially stressed and stonewashed to create patches and holes which expose the flesh and grab attention. Rather than being made to last, these clothes are nearly worn out before they are sold!

Clothes made in the sweatshops of poor countries where workers are paid poorly and exploited with long hours in pitiful conditions may give the illusion of being good clothes, but actually they are tamasic. The impact of such mass-produced clothes being moved around the world, to be cut in one country, stitched in another and zipped in yet another, is devastating to the environment. The excessive use of fossil fuels in doing this is causing global warming, and can be described in no other terms than tamasic. Cloth made from oil-based materials such as nylon, acrylic, polyester etc. is also tamasic, as the impact of such cloth may be injurious to both health and the environment in the long term, though invisible in the short term.

Such materials are intrinsically alien to the body, unfriendly to the touch and irritating to the skin. Sattvic fabrics have an immediate relationship with the body—wool attracts us for being warm and cosy in winter, while cotton is refreshing in the heat of summer. The design is easy and comfortable, allowing the body to be itself, rather than controlling its shape or exaggerating certain aspects. Sattvic clothes celebrate and enhance each particular body's own shape, gestures and movements.

The Three Qualities of Power

ULTIMATELY THESE THREE GUNAS are related to our state of mind. They live in the inner heart more than in outer appearances. One may live outwardly like a very simple person, possessing nothing but a loincloth and a thatched hut, but inwardly, that person may be full of ego, lust, anger, attachments and hatred. On the face of it, it may appear that such a person is a living example of a sattvic person, but the reality may be otherwise.

On the other hand, one may be a wealthy person, inheriting status, prestige and possessions, but be inwardly humble, detached and full of love for all living beings. On the face of it, such a person appears to be rajasic, but in reality that person is truly sattvic and serene.

In other words, a certain outward appearance, whether it is of poverty or of riches, could be given by two people who are of very different inner states of being.

Both a rajasic person and a sattvic person may possess power. So what distinguishes the power which a rajasic person exercises from that of a sattvic person? There is a story which answers this question.

Once upon a time, in the kingdom of Mithila, in northern India, lived a king called Janaka. He loved the land, forests, rivers, people and animals. He did not accept any remuneration for his royal duties from the state treasury. He managed all the affairs of the state as an act of service to his people. For his own livelihood he ploughed the land, threshed the rice and milked the cows. As a royal duty he participated in the ceremonies, rituals and courts of justice.

One day, in heaven, the god Vishnu praised King Janaka as a man of sattvic heart. Listening to this praise, one of Vishnu's attendants, a heavenly being, said sceptically, "Surely a king, with so much pomp and prestige, is rajasic—that is why he is called 'Raja'! How could he be called sattvic when he leads such a rajasic life? I cannot believe that he can free himself of rajasic qualities and at the same time live the royal life."

Vishnu replied, "Why don't you go and find out for yourself?"

So the heavenly being took the form of a Brahmin priest, descended to the earth and presented himself to King Janaka in a field by the River Ganga, where he was staying in a farmhouse.

"Welcome, holy man!" Janaka said. "What brings you here? May I offer you some lovely fresh mangos?"

"Yes, sir. I would be delighted to taste the famous mangos of this land. Sir, are you the king of this land? How far does your kingdom stretch? Where does your kingdom end?"

King Janaka replied, "The land does not belong to me, I belong to the land. How can anyone be King of Nature?"

The priest looked towards the capital city in the distance, and asked, "Then, are you the king of your capital city, and its people?"

"Maybe I am."

The priest, with his magical powers, created an illusion whereby it seemed as if the city, Janakpuri, was in flames, enveloped by a terrible fire with the sky above thick with black smoke. It was completely beyond rescue. Janaka looked at the burning city and said, "If I was truly the king of the capital, I would be able to control the flames and save its people. No, it cannot be that I am the king of the city. The earth and the elements obey their own laws and no human being can be king over them. We are all governed by the laws of the universe."

"Then, why are you called the King? Are you the king of your body then?" the priest persisted.

King Janaka paused for a moment and then said, "Perhaps I am. But then, do I have control over my body? My body becomes old and sick of its own accord. Can I stop death from taking away my body? No I cannot. And so I am not even king of my body, I am no king at all. I am part of the great flow of life. And we all play our part in this flow. You and I play our roles in this divine drama, the *lila*, of the universe."

The priest was so moved by the words of King Janaka that he revealed his true form as a heavenly being and bowing, said, "O great one, you have recognised the Truth, you have realised the ultimate essence of existence, you are free of cravings and desires to control and rule over others. I salute you. Even the gods in heaven are praising your integrity and your sattvic nature."

"Is that so!" said King Janaka in surprise. The power of sattvic people, like that of King Janaka, does not arise from the throne they occupy or the office they hold, or the outer appearance they project. It is an inner power which earns them the love and respect of others, and it is a power which in turn empowers others. They do not exercise power over others, but inspire others to discover and develop their own inner power.

King Janaka stands in a long line of individuals who held such an inner power, like the Buddha, Jesus Christ, Mahatma Gandhi, Martin Luther King and the Dalai Lama. They and many other sattvic leaders continue to influence the hearts and minds of millions of people, not through the power of their office but through their spiritual power.

Rajasic rulers would love to have such a genuine influence over other people, but cannot because they lack that soul power. Obsessed as they are with imposing their control, they lose control altogether. Paradoxically, those who renounce power over others become truly powerful, and those who seek power lose real power.

Even those who live a rajasic life can incorporate sattvic attitudes, values and practices. We can all try to avoid, if not altogether eliminate, tamasic tendencies from our lives. It is not important to judge where we are on the scale at any particular moment; what is important is the direction we face and the path we follow.

The End of Anguish

WHEN WE LOOK AT the modern world through the 'spiritual compass' of the three gunas, we find that rajasic ideologies have become the dominant values underpinning most of our actions, decisions and policies on the personal, political or social level.

Paradoxically, most of us seem to desire sattvic outcomes, such as beautiful surroundings, good health and a contented existence, but are attracted by the rajasic, which looks glamorous and exciting with promises of a wonderful future, with short cuts and quick-fix methods.

Thus we are anguished by our desire to achieve sattvic ends by using rajasic means. For example, we want to achieve peace, but pursue the path of war (which is rajasic descending into the tamasic). We want happiness, but follow the rajasic path of materialism, power and money. We want to achieve community cohesion, but follow the rajasic temptation of self-interest. Thus we keep sinking deeper and deeper into personal frustration and political misery.

What is the solution? It is to recognise that rajasic means cannot achieve sattvic ends.

There is no single solution to our manifold sufferings. We cannot be free from the problem of anguish as long as we look for one great answer imposed from above. Genuine or sattvic solutions are multiple solutions, emerging and unfolding from inside out, from the bottom up. Anguish will end when we stop trying to control and impose solutions from outside.

We need to be free of the rajasic ambition for dramatic and grand answers or miracle cures. What will work is something that emerges from within each situation, as a tree emerges from a seed. Sattvic methods are humble. They move slowly but surely, and develop step by step. For example, we cannot impose democracy on a country from outside. Appropriate forms of democracy and governance have to emerge and develop from within countries and communities, reflecting their local genius.

The three gunas can be a compass in our personal lives too. They can help to evaluate what would be the most appropriate form of action for an individual, according to his or her own true nature and deepest needs. If we followed our deepest needs, then we might decide, for example, to have a smaller house with a larger garden, instead of a glamorous flat in a fashionable and expensive district. We might choose to work near where we live with a smaller income, giving us more time for ourselves, our family and our friends, rather than to commute long distances for higher salaries or greater prestige.

Only each one of us can know our own innate sattvic qualities and develop them from within as an unfolding process. Our deepest needs will be revealed through our own inner voice. Obeying the expectations of others or attempting to meet the demands of society against our true nature and against our inner voice can only lead to frustration.

The genuine, sattvic way of living can only emerge from within, respecting the nature of reality, and following it with humility.

Of course, social or spiritual ideals expounded by great teachers or powerful books may evoke a response and act as a match to light the candle, but the ability to give light has to be in the candle itself; the nature of the response has to come from within. It cannot be imposed from without.

This is why most philosophers both in the East and the West have spoken of the need to 'know thyself'. Once we recognise and begin to live our own true nature, we are on the sattvic path. When we deviate from our own true nature, we fall into the rajasic and tamasic trap. So, ultimately, the sattvic quest is to seek the truth: know yourself and be your true self. By accepting ourselves as we are we discover our own true genius and find joy and happiness within our own creativity, spirituality and imagination.

The true nature of the soul is sattvic, which is beyond good and bad, beyond all colours. As the elements of earth, air, fire, water and space are beyond the moral distinctions of good and bad, so too is the essence of all beings.

Thus the purpose of the Ayurvedic discourse is to show that health and wholeness resides in being true to oneself. As Shakespeare wrote:

> This above all; to thine own self be true
> And it must follow, as the night the day,
> Thou canst not then be false to any man.

The three qualities present us with a stark choice, and of course the Ayurvedic masters teach us to choose the sattvic way of life, which is a way of elegant simplicity and profound spirituality.

Having described the meaning and scope of the three qualities, in the following chapters I will concentrate on the importance of sattva as a spiritual quality.

The Guest House

This being human is a guest house
Every morning a new arrival.

A joy, a depression, a meanness
Some momentary awareness comes
As an unexpected visitor.

Welcome and entertain them all
Even if they're a crowd of sorrows
Who violently sweep your house
Empty of its furniture.

Still treat each guest honourably;
He may be clearing you out
For some new delight.

The dark thought, the shame, the malice,
Meet them at the door laughing
And invite them in.

Be grateful for whoever comes,
Because each has been sent
As a guide from beyond.

Jallaludin Rumi

Chapter Two

SATTVIC SPIRIT: SPIRIT AND MATTER

The End of Dualism

Seek the spirit, but not out of spiritual lust
or spiritual egoism;
Seek it rather because you want to become selfless
in the practical life of the material world.
Spirit is never without matter, matter is never without spirit!
We will do everything material in the light of the spirit,
and we will seek the light of the spirit in such a way that it
enkindles warmth in us for our practical deeds.
Rudolf Steiner

SATTVIC IS SPIRITUAL; but when we think of the spiritual we are caught in the illusion that spiritual is anti-material, which is not the case. Matter and spirit are two sides of the same coin. What we measure is matter, what we feel is spirit. Matter represents quantity while spirit represents quality. Spirit manifests itself through matter whereas matter comes to life through spirit.

Spirit brings meaning to matter, matter gives form to spirit. Without spirit, matter lacks life. We are human body and human spirit at the same time. A tree, too, has body and spirit; even rocks, which appear to be dead, contain their own spirit. There is no dichotomy, no dualism, no separation between matter and spirit.

The problem is not matter but 'materialism'. Similarly, the problem is not spirit but 'spiritualism'. The moment we encapsulate an idea or a thought into an 'ism', we lay the foundations of dualistic thought. Let all 'isms' become 'wasms'! The universe is uni-verse, one song, one verse, one poem. It contains infinite forms which dance together in harmony, sing together in concert, balance each other in gravity, transform each other in evolution, and yet the universe maintains its wholeness and its implicate order. Dark and light, above and below, left and right, words and meaning, matter and spirit, complement each other, comfortable in mutual embrace. Where is the contradiction? Where is the conflict?

Life feeds life, matter feeds matter, and spirit feeds spirit. Life feeds matter, matter feeds life and spirit feeds both matter and life. There is total reciprocity. This is the composite sattvic worldview, practised in the traditions of the pre-industrial culture of India, where matter and spirit are in eternal reciprocity and harmony.

Modern dualistic cultures see nature as red in tooth and claw, the strongest and fittest surviving, the weak and meek disappearing, and conflict and competition as the only true life structure. From this worldview emerges the notion of a split between mind and matter. Once mind and matter are split, debate ensues as to whether mind is superior to matter or matter is superior to mind.

This rajasic worldview of split, rift, conflict, competition, separation and dualism has also given birth to the idea of separation between the human and the natural world. This has reinforced the rather arrogant, self-appointed superiority of the human species, which authorises people to control and manipulate nature for their use. In this view of the world, nature exists for human benefit alone. According to this 'utilitarian' view, the natural world—plants, animals, rivers, oceans, mountains and skies—are denuded of their own inherent spirit and intrinsic value. Their value is perceived only in the context of their usefulness to humans. If spirit exists at all, then it is limited to the human spirit. But even that is doubtful. Within this rajasic worldview, humans are nothing more than formations of molecules, genes and four elements. Mind is a function of the brain, and the brain is an organ in the head and no more.

This rajasic notion of spiritless existence can be described as materialism. All is matter: land, forests, food, water, labour, literature and art are commodities to be bought and sold in the marketplace—the world market, the stock-market and the so-called 'free' market. This is a market of competitive advantage, a cut-throat market, a market where the survival of the fittest is the greatest imperative—the strong competing with the weak and winning the biggest share of the market for themselves. Ironically, monopolies are established in the name of free competition. Five supermarket chains control 80 percent of the food sold in the UK. Four or five giant multinational corporations control 80 percent of the international food trade. Small sattvic family farms cannot compete with the big rajasic players, and are forced to declare defeat. This is a world where spirit has been driven out. Business without spirit, trade without compassion, industry without ecology, finance without fairness and economics without equity can only be described as rajasic, leading toward tamasic and resulting in the breakdown of society and destruction of the natural world. Only when spirit and business work together can we call it sattvic business.

JUST AS MATERIALISM, derived from rajasic and tamasic tendencies, rules economics, it also rules politics. Instead of seeing the nations, regions and cultures of the world as one human community, the world is divided into a battlefield of nations competing with each other for power, influence and control over minds, markets and natural resources. One nation's interest is seen as being in opposition to the national interest of another: Indian national interest is opposed to Pakistani national interest and vice versa; Palestinian national interest is opposed to Israeli national interest; American national interest versus Iraqi national interest; Chechen national interest versus Russian national interest and so on. We have polarised politics: 'If you are not with us, you are against us' has become the dominant mindset. And if you are not with us, you are not only against us, you are part of the global axis of evil. This is tamasic politics, denuded of spirit. What can we expect from such politics other than rivalry, strife, the arms race, nuclear proliferation, terrorism and wars? Politicians speak of democracy and freedom, but they pursue the path of hegemony and self-interest. How can a particular view of democracy and freedom suit the whole world? There can be no democracy and freedom without compassion, reverence and respect for diversity and pluralism. Compassion, reverence and respect are sattvic qualities—but politics founded on materialism considers the sattvic values of the spirit to be woolly, flaky, utopian, idealistic, unrealistic and irrational. However, it is worth asking where the tamasic politics of power, control and self-interest have led us. The two world wars, the Cold War, the Vietnam war, the war in Kashmir, Iraq and the attack on the Twin Towers of New York, to name a few. Tamasic politics has proved to be a grand failure, and therefore it is time to practise sattvic politics by bringing politics and spirituality together again.

SOMETIMES THE WORDS 'spirituality' and 'religion' are confused, but they are not the same thing. The word religion comes from the Latin root *religo*, which means 'bind together'. People come together in a group, share a belief system, stick together and support each other. Thus religion binds you, whereas the root meaning of 'spirit' is associated with breath, with air. We can all be free spirits and breathe freely. Spirituality transcends beliefs. The spirit moves, inspires, touches our hearts and refreshes our souls.

When a room has been left closed, with the doors and windows shut and curtains drawn for a few days, the air becomes stale. When we enter such a room we find it stuffy, so we open the doors and windows to bring in fresh air. In the same way, when minds are closed for too long we need a radical avatar or teacher to open the windows so that our stuffy minds and stale thoughts are aired again. A Buddha, a Jesus, a Gandhi, a Rumi, a Hildegard of Bingen appears to help us to blow away the cobwebs of our closed minds. Of course, we do not need to wait for such prophets; we can be our own prophets, unlock our own hearts and minds and allow the fresh air of compassion, of generosity, of divinity, of sacredness to blow through our lives.

However, religious groups and traditions have an important role to play. They initiate us into a discipline of thought and practice, they provide us with a framework, and they offer us a sense of community, of solidarity, of support. A tender seedling needs a pot and a stick to support it in the early stages of its development, or even the enclosure of a nursery to protect it from frost and cold winds. But when it is strong enough it needs to be planted out in the open so that it is able to develop its own roots and become a fully mature tree. Likewise, religious orders act as nurseries for seeking souls. But in the end, we each need to establish our own roots and find our own sattvic way of life.

Religion is made up of four dimensions, one of them rajasic and the rest sattvic.

There is the *institutional* dimension where we adhere to an organisation, to a set of rules. These institutions can be a help or a hindrance depending on the way we use them. The churches, temples, mosques and synagogues, the books and scriptures—all these aspects are part of institutionalised religions. There is a strong element of pomp and power in these institutions, and they are run on rajasic patterns.

The second dimension of religion is *aesthetic*. All religions have developed delightful forms of music, lovely architecture, inspiring poetry and paintings, beautiful rituals and ceremonies. They ignite our imagination. They give us joy and a sense of beauty. Without this aesthetic dimension, religions are impoverished.

Then there is the *ethical* dimension. Love your neighbour, love your enemy, be a good Samaritan, practise selfless service and diminish your ego. These are ethical teachings, bringing us freedom from greed, anger and pride, liberation from delusion, cravings and grasping, and the ability to see the interconnectedness and interdependence of all life. These sattvic, ethical teachings bring us contentment, fulfilment, satisfaction, happiness and self-realisation at a personal level, and a shared vision and common values at the social level.

Then there is the fourth dimension, which is *mystical*. Every religious tradition has a mystical component: Sufism among Muslims, the Kabbalah in Jewish tradition, Bhakti yoga (the practice of the devotional path) for Hindus, and the teachings of St John of the Cross, St Francis and Hildegard of Bingen among the Christians. All these mystic traditions experience the presence of the divine all around them. They practise complete and utter dedication to the divine. There is nothing else but the divine.

This sattvic, mystical experience is rooted in a sense of the sacred. At present, the institutional aspect of religion has become dominant and other aspects are either undervalued or seen as secondary. The true strength of religion is not in large rajasic institutions. The aesthetic, ethical and mystical aspects are the backbone of all religions. The institutions are there only to facilitate the mystical, ethical and aesthetic experiences of individuals and communities.

Religious institutions need to remain small and flexible so that the sattvic qualities of aesthetics, ethics and mysticism can be practised freely by all members of a religious tradition.

There are many religions, philosophies and traditions. Respecting them all means accepting that different religious traditions meet the needs of different people, at different times, in different places and in different contexts. This spirit of generosity, inclusivity and recognition is a sattvic quality. Whenever religious orders lose this quality, they become no more than rajasic sects protecting their vested interests.

Institutionalised religions have fallen into the rajasic trap. For them, the maintenance of institutions has become more important than helping their members to grow, to develop and discover their own free spirit. When religious orders become obsessed with maintaining their properties and their institutions they lose their spirituality, becoming in effect businesses without spirit. Just as it is necessary to restore spirit in business and politics, the spirit needs to be restored in religion. This may seem a strange proposition, because the very *raison d'être* of every religion is to seek the spirit. But, the reality is otherwise. Religions have done a lot of good, but they have also done a lot of harm. We can see all around us the tension between religious institutions. These tensions are major causes of conflicts, wars and disharmony. Rivalry among religions would cease if they realised that, despite their differing theologies, they are like rivers flowing into the same great ocean of spirituality, providing the sattvic quality of refreshment. There is no conflict among rivers. Why then should there be conflict among religions? Respect for diversity of beliefs is a spiritual imperative.

AS BUSINESS, POLITICS and religious institutions need to return to their spiritual roots in order to find a sense of the sattvic, so the environmental and social justice movements need to embrace a spiritual dimension to establish sattvic ecology and sattvic justice. At present, most social change movements concentrate on negative campaigning. They present doom and gloom scenarios and become mirror images of the institutions they criticise.

The real impetus for ecological sustainability and social justice stems from an ethical, aesthetic and spiritual vision. But when campaigners and activists forget the real reasons for their social engagement and become trapped by media glamour and the fame that goes with it, or lose the larger picture in proposals, reports, mobilising or lobbying, the very purpose of their work becomes diluted. These concerns become ends in themselves and annihilate a holistic, inclusive and constructive vision. Love of nature and the intrinsic value of all life—human as well as other than human—is the sattvic ground in which environmental and social justice movements need to be rooted. The basis of all campaigning is to restore a sense of reverence for life, and this is a spiritual basis. There is no contradiction between pragmatic campaigning and the quest for meaning. Gandhi's political programme was founded on spiritual values, and so was Martin Luther King's civil rights movement. Contemporary environmental and social justice movements also require that sattvic worldview, rather than being attracted to the rajasic work of building big organisational structures.

IT IS OFTEN BELIEVED that science and spirituality are like oil and water—they cannot mix. This is a rajasic notion. Science needs spirituality and spirituality needs science. When science overrides all restraint—moral, ethical and ecological—and strives to achieve everything that is achievable, experimenting with everything irrespective of the consequences, then it leads to the tamasic technologies of nuclear weapons, genetic engineering, human and animal cloning and poisonous products which pollute the soil, water and air. It is dangerous to give science *carte blanche* to dominate human minds and to subjugate the natural world. Contemporary science has acquired such a status of superiority that it commands the total obeisance of industry, business, education and politics. Some of its experiments have become so crude and cruel that they contradict the very term 'civilisation'. We need ethical and ecological values to keep ever-striding science reined in, and not allow it to destroy itself with its tamasic power.

As science needs spirituality, so spirituality also needs science. Without a certain amount of rational, analytical and intellectual skill, spirituality can easily turn into woolly cults and sectarian pursuits. There is no dualism between science and the spirit. Spirituality is not just for saints, or confined to monastic orders or caves in the mountains. Spirituality is in everyday life. Ordinary activities such as growing food, cooking, eating, washing up, sweeping the floor, building, making clothes and caring for neighbours are spiritual, if performed with sattvic motivation and mindfulness. We need to bring spirituality into all parts of our lives: into politics, into business, into agriculture and into education. And we must do so with a scientific approach.

WE HUMAN BEINGS have our physical needs and also our spiritual needs. Food, water, shelter, warmth, work, education and health are our physical needs. We need to engage in economic activities to fulfil these needs. But once these needs are met, we need to find a sense of contentment and the wisdom to know when enough is enough. If we go on multiplying our economic activities even after our essential physical needs are met, then we become unhappy victims of greed and desire. Many of our social, political and environmental crises are crises of desire.

Those who profit from endless economic growth put enormous effort into persuading us that by having more material goods we shall be happy. But happiness does not come from material things. They can give us convenience and physical comfort. We need material things for material needs but we also have social, psychological and spiritual needs—the need for community, for love, for friendship, for beauty, for art and music. We need non-material things to feed our imagination and our creativity. We need the opportunity to make things with our own hands. We need time to be still and contemplate, we need spaces to appreciate and enjoy. These are spiritual needs. They cannot be met by accumulating more and more material goods. It is important to differentiate between physical and spiritual needs and to understand that things which can satisfy physical needs are incapable of satisfying spiritual needs, and vice versa.

Materialism in its extreme form is tamasic and is obviously untenable. If the six billion citizens of the world were to live the materialistic lifestyle of Western societies, we would need six planets! But we do not have six planets, we have only one. Therefore we need to invent a sattvic lifestyle of elegant simplicity, where the Earth's gifts are shared among all human beings fairly without short-changing the non-human world.

We embrace simplicity not only because the consumerist lifestyle is unfair, unjust and unsustainable but also because it is the cause of discontent, dissatisfaction, disharmony, depression, disease and division. Even if there were no problems of global warming, resource shortage, pollution and waste, we would still need to choose a simpler lifestyle that is conducive to and congruent with equity, aesthetics, happiness and spirituality. A lifestyle uncluttered by the burden of unnecessary possessions is the sattvic lifestyle of boundless joy.

The Buddha was a prince; he owned palaces, elephants, horses, land, gold and silver. Soon he realised that all his wealth was holding him back and creating a mirage of happiness. Further, it was keeping him chained to greed, desire, craving, pride, ego, fear and anger. So he embraced a life of noble poverty. This kind of poverty meant a voluntary acceptance of limits. This was not because of a population explosion at that time, nor a shortage of raw materials or natural resources.

There was no global warming at that time. Yet he preferred the sattvic path of elegant simplicity because the sattvic way was the right way to meet the needs of the soul as well as the body.

MY LAND, MY HOUSE, *my* possessions, *my* power, *my* wealth—these are the stuff of small minds. Spirituality frees us from the small mind and liberates us from the small 'I', the ego identity. Through spirituality we are able to open the doors of the big mind and big heart where sharing, caring and compassion come naturally. Life exists only through the gift of the 'other'—all life is interdependent. Existence is an intricately interconnected web of relationships where we all share the same breath of life. Whether we are rich or poor, black or white, young or old, humans or animals, fish or fowl, trees or rocks, everything is sustained by the same air, the same sunshine, the same water, the same soil. There are no boundaries, no borders, no separation, no divisions, no duality; it is all the dance of eternal life where spirit and matter dance together. Day and night dance together, and wherever there is the dance of life, there is joy and beauty.

However, the religion of materialism and the culture of consumerism that have been promoted by rajasic civilisation have blocked the flow of joy and beauty. Once Mahatma Gandhi was asked, "What do you think of Western civilisation?" He replied, "I think it would be a good idea!"

Yes, it would be a good idea, because any society which goes to war to control oil or produces nuclear weapons to maintain its political power, discarding all values of the spirit, cannot be called a civilisation. How can a greedy consumerist culture built on an unfair, unjust and unsustainable economic system be called civilised? The true mark of civilisation is to maintain a balance between material progress and spiritual integrity. At the very least, how can we consider ourselves to be civilised when nations, cultures and religions cannot even live with each other in harmony? We have developed technologies to reach the Moon, but not the wisdom to live with our neighbours. A civilisation without a spiritual foundation is no civilisation at all.

The way we treat animals is a clear example of a lack of civilisation. Cows, pigs and chickens live as prisoners in factory farms; mice, monkeys and rabbits in laboratories are treated as if they feel no pain. We believe that all life is expendable to pander to human desire. Racism, nationalism, sexism and ageism have been challenged and to some extent mitigated, but 'humanism' still governs us. As a result, we consider the human species to be superior to all others. This humanism is a kind of 'species-ism'.

To create the civilisation of Mahatma Gandhi's dream we need a spiritual revolution. So where do we begin? We begin with ourselves. Self-transformation is the first step towards social, political and spiritual transformation. All transformations start at the bottom and move upwards to embrace the larger world. That is the law of the natural world. The mighty oak begins with the sowing of an acorn in the soil. After the seed is sown, for a few weeks or months no one knows whether it is living or dead, or whether it will ever emerge into the world. But that unseen transformation under the earth's surface enables the acorn to emerge out of the soil as a tiny, tender shoot. It is still small and insignificant, but the mighty oak begins from that insignificance.

So social and political transformation grows out of the seeds of personal transformation. When we are free from fear and anxiety, and are at ease with ourselves, then we are able to engage with the community around us. That act of personal engagement in turn brings us a greater sense of fulfilment in a wonderful dovetailing of the personal, the social and the political.

Three Sattvic Virtues

TRUST: NOW I WOULD like to explore three sattvic virtues which can help us to bring about a spiritual revolution. First and foremost among them is to cultivate *trust*. If we look deep into ourselves, we will see that fear is at the root of consumerism and materialism. Insecurity, ambition, the desire for power and control, the eagerness to prove ourselves and impress others, addiction to shopping—all these tamasic emotions are related to fear. Personal insecurity expands into social and political insecurity.

So the first step towards spiritual renewal is to look at the phenomenon of fear in our lives. Fear breeds fear. We go to great lengths to build psychological and physical defences, but they only increase our fear. Even when some nations have nuclear weapons to protect them, they are not free from fear. History has proved that nuclear weapons bring no permanent security. The attack on the twin towers of the World Trade Centre in New York proved that a knife or a razor blade can equally be a weapon of attack, so where is the justification for spending so much effort, time and resources building nuclear warheads when they actually bring no security? The most powerful country in the world, the USA, is also the most insecure country in the world. Paradoxically, the more defences we build, the more insecure we are. Shielding oneself has a paralysing effect. Therefore the first step is to examine the tamasic nature of fear.

The antidote to fear is trust. Trust yourself: you are good the way you are. Irrespective of who you are, you embody, all at the same time, a divine spark, a creative impulse and the power of imagination. These will always be with you and protect you. Trust others—they are in the same boat as you. They long for love as much as you do. Only in relationships with others will you blossom. You are because others are and others are because you are. We all exist, flourish, blossom and mature in this mutuality, this reciprocity, and the web of relationships. Give love and it will be reciprocated. Give fear, and it too will be reciprocated. Sow one seed of thistle and you will get hundreds of thorny thistles. Sow one seed of camellia and you will get hundreds of camellias. You will reap what you sow—this is the old wisdom, and yet we have not learned it.

Then trust the process of the universe. We have the sun to nourish all life; we have water to quench our thirst and soil to grow food. We have trees to bear fruit and mothers' milk to feed babies. The process of the universe is embedded in the life-support system of mutuality.

Hundreds of millions of species are all fed, watered, sheltered and taken care of by this mysterious process—trust it. As St Julian of Norwich said, "All shall be well; all manner of things shall be well." Do no harm, you will not be harmed. Trust is the first sattvic virtue.

PARTICIPATION: THE SECOND SATTVIC virtue is *participation*. Participate in the magical process of life. Life is a miracle; we cannot explain it, nor can we know it in full, but we can actively and consciously participate in it without trying to control, manipulate or subjugate it.

Participation is simple. We have been given two wonderful hands to cultivate the soil and grow food. Working with the soil in the garden meets the need of the body as much as the need of the spirit. Industrial farming has taken away our birthright to participate in the cultivation of food. Large-scale, mechanised and industrialised farming is born of our desire to dominate the land. Small-scale, natural, local farming—still better, gardening—is a way of participation with the rhythms of the seasons. Ideally land should be gardened not farmed. Animals should be freed from the prisons of factory farms. Growing food is one example of the sattvic principle of participation. Cooking food and sharing that food with family, friends and guests are as much spiritual activities as they are social and economic activities. Fast food has taken away from us the fundamental activity of participation in the daily ritual of handling and preparing food. The Italian Slow Food movement is a great attempt to counter this trend. Slow food is sattvic food. Fast food is tamasic food.

Slowness is a spiritual quality. If we wish to participate properly in the process of life and restore our spirituality, we have to slow down. Paradoxically, it is only when we go slower that we can go further. Doing less, consuming less, producing less will enable us to *be* 'more'—to celebrate more, to enjoy more. Time is what makes things perfect. Give yourself time to make things and give yourself time to rest. Take time to 'do' as well as to 'be'. It is in the participation in this dance of doing and being that spirituality is to be found.

Once the Emperor of Persia asked his Sufi master, "Please advise me, what should I be doing to renew my soul, revive my spirit and refresh my mind, so that I can be happy in myself and effective in my work?"

The Sufi master replied, "My Lord, sleep as long as you can!"

The Emperor was surprised, "Sleep? I have little time to sleep," he said with irritation. "I have justice to dispense, laws to enact, ambassadors to receive and armies to command. How can I sleep when I have so much to do?"

The Sufi master replied, "My Lord, the longer you sleep the less you will oppress!"

The Emperor was speechless; he saw the sage's point. He conceded that the sage was blunt but right.

Modern societies are like the Emperor of Persia. The longer we work, the more we consume—we drive cars, fly in planes, burn electricity, go shopping and produce waste. The faster we do these things the more damage we inflict on the environment, on the poor and on our own peace of mind. Speed leads to control; slowness to participation. True participation is to live and work in harmony with ourselves, with others and with the natural world. Participation is not about speed and efficiency, it is about harmony, balance and appropriateness of action.

GRATITUDE: THE THIRD SATTVIC virtue is *gratitude*. In modern life we complain about everything. If it is raining, we say, 'Isn't the weather awful—so wet and cold!' When it is sunny we complain, 'Isn't it hot, so hot!' The media are full of cynicism, complaints and criticism. Debates in parliaments are mostly negative. The Opposition blames the Government and the Government complains about the Opposition. This national pastime of blaming permeates even into our families and workplaces. Because of the tamasic culture of condemnation, we learn to condemn ourselves too. 'I am not good enough' is a widespread feeling. 'I should be doing something different, something else, something better.' 'I had a terrible childhood,' we complain. 'My school was awful,' we moan. 'I'm never appreciated by my colleagues,' we grumble, and this kind of grumbling goes on interminably.

In order to grow spiritually, we need to develop the sattvic faculty of appreciation and gratitude. We need to train ourselves to recognise the gifts we have received from our ancestors, our parents, our teachers, our colleagues and our society in general. We also need to express our thankfulness for the gifts of the Earth. What a wonderful Gaian system it is! It regulates climate, it organises the seasons and provides an abundance of nourishment, beauty, sensual pleasure, and spiritual fulfilment to all creatures. When we are in awe and wonder at the workings of the earth, we cannot but feel blessed and grateful. When food is served, we are filled with a sense of gratitude. We thank the cook and the farmer, but we ought also to thank the soil, rain and sunshine. We should even express our gratitude to the earthworms that have been working day and night to keep the soil fertile. However green a gardener's fingers may be, there will be no food without the worms. So in praise we should say, 'Long live the worms!' We join the poet Gerard Manley Hopkins and say, "Long live the wet and the wilderness yet." It is the beauty of the wild that feeds our soul while the fruit of the Earth feeds the body.

The generosity and unconditional love of the Earth for all its creatures is boundless. We plant one small seed of an apple in the ground. That tiny seed results in a tree within a few years and eventually produces thousands and thousands of apples year after year. And all that from a tiny pip, sometimes self-sown. The tree knows no discrimination, asks no questions. It offers its fruit to poor or rich, saint or sinner, fool or philosopher, wasp or bird. What else can we feel for the tree but gratitude? And from our gratitude flows humility. Arrogance comes from complaining and criticism. When we are critical of nature we come to the conclusion that it needs technology and engineering, and embark upon improving it—but end up destroying it.

IN THE SATTVIC WORLDVIEW there is no dualism, no separation between matter and spirit. Spirit is held within matter, and matter within spirit. However, because of the dominance of the rajasic mode of living, we have separated them and made spirit a private matter, and have allowed matter to dominate our public life. We need to heal this rift urgently. Without such healing the material world will continue to suffer catastrophic consequences, and the spirit will also suffer because it will be seen as idealistic, esoteric and otherworldly—irrelevant to our everyday existence.

When we are able to heal this rift, we will be able to instil spirit in business and create a sattvic economy. We will be able to create sattvic politics that work for all. Our religions will become a source of healing. The movement for environmental sustainability and social justice will inspire millions to live a sattvic life. Then human beings will be at ease with themselves and with the world around them. This marriage of matter and spirit, of business and spirit, of politics and spirit, of religion and spirit and of activism and spirit is the greatest union required in our time in order to establish a sattvic culture.

Human beings are made of body and spirit. Once their bodily needs are met, they long for inner fulfilment through peace, love and creativity. People are hungry for nourishment of the soul. Therefore, the great work we have in our hands is to create space and time for people to discover the unity of body and spirit.

Similarly a tree is not just timber. We need to see the physical and metaphysical dimensions of trees simultaneously. The speaking tree, the tree of knowledge and the tree of life express the implicit spiritual quality of the tree. We need to move from the rajasic quality of dualism and separation to the sattvic quality of wholeness, integrity and relatedness.

The Mystery of Life

The ideals which have lighted my way, and time after time, have given me new courage to face life cheerfully, have been Kindness, Beauty and Truth.

The trite objects of human efforts—possessions, outward success, luxury—have always seemed to me contemptible.

The most beautiful experience we can have is the mysterious. It is the fundamental emotion which stands at the cradle of true art and true science. It was the experience of mystery—even if mixed with fear—that engendered religion. A knowledge of the existence of something we cannot penetrate, our perceptions of the profoundest reason and the most radiant beauty, which only in their most primitive forms are accessible to our minds—it is this knowledge and this emotion that constitute true religiosity; in this sense, and in this alone, I am a deeply religious man. I cannot conceive of a God who rewards and punishes his creatures, or has a will of the kind that we experience in ourselves. Neither can I nor would I want to conceive of an individual that survives his physical death; let feeble souls, from fear or absurd egoism, cherish such thoughts. I am satisfied with the mystery of the eternity of life and with the awareness and a glimpse of the marvellous structure of the existing world, together with the devoted striving to comprehend a portion, be it ever so tiny, of the Reason that manifests itself in nature.

Albert Einstein

Interbeing

There is a cloud floating in this sheet of paper that you are holding in your hand. Without a cloud, there will be no rain; without rain, the trees cannot grow; and without trees, we cannot make paper. The cloud is essential for the paper to exist. If the cloud is not here, the sheet of paper cannot be here either; so the cloud and the paper inter-are.

If we look into this sheet of paper even more deeply, we can see the sunshine in it. If the sunshine is not there, the forest cannot grow. In fact, nothing can grow. Even we cannot grow without sunshine. And so, we know that the sunshine is also in this sheet of paper; the paper and the sunshine inter-are.

And if we continue to look, we can see the logger who cut the tree and brought it to the mill to be transformed into paper. And we see the wheat. We know the logger cannot exist without his daily bread, and therefore the wheat that became his bread is also in this sheet of paper. And the logger's father and mother are in it too.

Looking even more deeply, we can see we are in it too, because when we look at a sheet of paper, the sheet of paper is part of our perception.

So everything is in this sheet of paper. You cannot point out one thing that is not here—time, space, the Earth, the rain, the minerals in the soil, the sunshine, the cloud, the river, the heat. Everything co-exists with this sheet of paper.

'To be' is 'to inter-be'. You cannot just be by yourself, alone. You have to inter-be with every other thing. This sheet of paper is, because everything else is. As thin as this sheet of paper is, it contains everything in the universe within it.

Thich Nhat Hanh

Chapter Three

THE SATTVIC WAY OF LIFE

Bread, Bees and Trees

THE SATTVIC QUALITY IS the only real tool we have which is going to take us through these difficult times. Without values, we cannot move in the right direction. Even gardening or farming, taking care of our family or our communities, all that work has to be done—not as a duty or a chore, not just to earn a living or to make ends meet, not just to pay the bills or pay the mortgage, but for joy. When we are gardening or performing any other action with joy, it becomes a sattvic practice; when we are taking care of the soil, we are taking care of our soul as well, if we do it with sattvic motivation. Care of the soil and care of the soul are not two separate things; they are two aspects of the same spiritual reality.

When I was a monk, at the age of eighteen I came across Mahatma Gandhi's autobiography. In it, he said that there are some people who leave the world and become monks. They live in monasteries or caves in the Himalayas and they see the world as a trap or as bondage. For them politics is dirty, business is dirty, industry is dirty; and they think that they should not get their hands dirty in the world and get caught in separation and rajasic dualism. So they live in a monastic order and they practise spirituality. On the other hand, the people who are living in the world think that spirituality is only for saints. They feel that they cannot practise spirituality in the world; they have to pay bills and the mortgage; how can they practise spirituality? Gandhi wanted to rescue religion from the religious elite. He believed that the practice of spirituality is not the monopoly of monks and mullahs, sadhus and saints; spirituality is the birthright of everyone.

Gandhi said that this division between spirituality and the world should end. We must bring spirituality into everyday life. It is not the preserve of someone who worships in a church, mosque or temple. We have to practise spirituality in politics, in industry, in business, in farming, in gardening, in raising children, and in bringing up a family. When we integrate spirituality into everyday life, it is transformed into sattvic life. When I read that book as a monk, I was shaken; I thought that Mahatma Gandhi was right, it made sense. I felt that what I was doing was totally the opposite. I was putting spirituality and everyday reality into two separate boxes. I could not sleep that night; I kept tossing and turning, and thinking that although outwardly, as a monk, I might appear to be a sattvic person, in separating the world and the spirit I was on a rajasic path. This proved to be a turning point; that night, after midnight when everyone was asleep, I escaped from the monastery and joined a Gandhian ashram. There I learned to integrate spirituality into everyday life.

Bread labour was considered a sattvic and a spiritual activity.

Baking bread is a simple example of spirituality in everyday life. People say, 'I do not have time to make bread.' Gandhi might reply, 'If you have no time to bake bread, then you have no time to live!' When Jesus Christ gave bread to his disciples at his Last Supper, he said, "This bread is my body, I am the bread." Now, when we go to Christian churches we are given a wafer—a white, factory-made, mass-produced wafer! A wafer to celebrate Mass! Is a wafer the body of Christ?

The significance of bread is realised not only by Christians, but by other religions as well. The Buddhist monk Thich Nhat Hanh has said, "The bread in your hand is the body of the cosmos." When you knead the dough, you feel a spiritual connection with the soil. When you are waiting for the dough to rise, you can be in meditation. Baking bread at home in a thoughtful manner is a sattvic activity. Such bread is a symbol of home, family and caring. Spirituality is nothing other than this caring quality of the soul.

Nowadays bread has become big business, but whether it is any good for us, we can no longer be sure. Gone are the days when the fresh smell of wholesome bread filled the kitchen, when every loaf of bread was different and when baking bread was an aesthetic experience.

Also gone are the days when we could walk to our local bakery and enjoy the sensual pleasure of seeing and smelling the freshly baked bread arranged on the wooden shelves, to chat with the baker and others from our neighbourhood. Those were the days when the bakery was the centre of the community. Now only a tiny proportion of bread in the UK is either home-made or baked in small, neighbourhood bakeries, and could be called sattvic bread.

Bread diversity was a symbol of cultural diversity. Regional varieties represented the diversity of grain as well as of style. We should be ashamed because the quality of bread has dramatically deteriorated over the years. Our bread is sterile. It is so devoid of any life that the manufacturers have to inject vitamins and minerals artificially into the bread they sell; even colour is added to make it look brown and wholesome. Yet, with massive advertising, people have been fooled into eating what is a national disgrace.

By paying attention to good bread we can combat companies which produce genetically engineered wheat, multinationals which patent seeds, and we can support small-scale, local and organic methods of wheat production as opposed to the monoculture of the American and Canadian prairies. How can we launch such a bread revolution? Perhaps we could have a Campaign for Real Bread, like the Campaign for Real Ale? We need to organise a boycott of factory bread. How about car stickers: 'Bring Back the Local Bakery' or 'Eat Real Bread' or 'Bake Your Own'?

Our schools would be good places to start. Good education cannot be provided on bad bread. Let every school teach children the art and science of baking. Let the school lunch be based on good bread. Baking bread is not a waste of time; it is the foundation of good education. Let learning be led by bread.

We need to begin with good sattvic bread if we wish to restore the health of the people and the planet. When we are mindful of the quality of bread, we will be mindful of the quality of food. When we are mindful of the quality of food, we will be mindful of the quality of life.

The quality of bread is too important to be left to bread manufacturers—their prime objective is to make profit, rather than to provide bread for health. Baking our own bread or buying bread baked at a small local bakery are the only two options which can free us from the monopolistic stranglehold of the big bread business. The first step towards autonomy of the individual and of the local community is to take back our basic right of access to good bread. A healthy loaf of bread is everybody's birthright.

AT THE GANDHIAN ASHRAM I learned that cultivating the soil is not just a way of producing food. Yes, that will happen, but it is also a way of cultivating the soul. Gardening is hard work; farming is hard work; building a house with your own hands is hard work. In our modern society we have come to believe that hard work is bad for you. Everything should be easy; it should be done by machine. But when you become addicted to the machine, you become addicted to mass production and mass consumption. All addictions are tamasic. The economics of addiction leads to war, climate change, depletion of the earth's resources and societal breakdown. What I learned from Gandhi was that by making things with my hands I not only produced vegetables or bread to eat, or the cloth I had spun or woven, or the shoes I had made, but I did all these activities as a creative expression of my imagination. In other words, living a simple and sattvic life is a spiritual practice; the work itself is prayer, a service to the land, a service to the soil, and when I am serving the land and the soil I am serving the universe. When I can see that all life upon the Earth is sacred, then I am filled with awe and wonder, with ecological humility.

In our modern way of thinking, we believe that human beings are somehow in charge of the Earth, that all land is created for human use, that the trees and forests exist for the benefit of humans. But in sattvic, humble thinking, we are one with the Earth and therefore we thank the Earth for everything that we receive from her as a gift. All species, humans and other than humans, are part of the same web of life. We are in a relationship with all species, with the Earth itself. When we use the gifts of the Earth with frugality and restraint, then our relationship with it is harmonious. Mass production and mass consumption are a form of tamasic arrogance. Making things by hand, taking little from the Earth, expressing our inner sense of beauty, creativity and aesthetics in what we make, avoiding waste and pollution and celebrating the Earth's abundance are all forms of a sattvic life.

Trees of Spirit

IN ADDITION TO BAKING BREAD with my own hands, I learned that to plant, care for and celebrate trees is one of the most simple, sattvic actions. 'Meditate on trees' was the motto of my mentor at the Ashram. The seed—less than a quarter of an inch long—is a miracle. Take an apple seed, for example. When you are eating an apple, you find a pip in it which is bitter, so you spit it out. That pip goes into the soil and grows into a plant; that seed sacrifices itself—lets go of its own identity, its own ego. Once planted, it is completely gone, biodegraded. We see no more of it. It becomes part of the soil, but out of its sacrifice a tree grows, and in a few years' time you get apples. You may not believe in reincarnation, but just observe the apple which you have grown. That seed which went into the soil and died many years ago is now reincarnated in that apple. The seed is reborn; that is reincarnation and not one, but two, three or four seeds are reborn. From one seed, hundreds and thousands of apples grow. What an abundance of life we have. That one apple seed went into the soil and died for us. It has also died for the benefit of the animals, birds and worms; in fact for the benefit of the entire Earth. No wonder people in India worship the tree. Trees are the teachers of the sattvic life.

Look at the unconditional love and generosity of that apple. Anyone can go to the tree and pick apples, completely free. The apple tree will never tell you that you cannot have an apple unless you have money or a credit card. The apple is unconditionally generous and loving. You can learn spirituality from the apple tree; it never discriminates—you can be a saint or a sinner, educated or uneducated, man or woman, black or white, Christian or Muslim, human or animal, bird or wasp—whoever you are, you can help yourself to an apple. There is no 'free lunch' in the market economy; it deals in commodities, everything is bought and sold: food, land, even water. But in nature, all the creatures on this planet have a free lunch—every day! They do not buy or sell, they do not need supermarkets to get their food. All creatures are fed and watered without any monetary exchange. Here is something we can learn from the self-organising system of nature.

Trees help to protect, save and serve all living things, from birds to insects, from humans to animals, all the organisms in the soil; everything receives life from a tree. So it is everybody's sattvic duty and sacred responsibility to serve the tree in return—humans, animals, birds and worms all owe it to the tree. This is a relationship of mutuality, of reciprocity and interdependence; we depend on trees and trees depend on us. In that way, like a child caring for parents, we take care of our tree as if it were our kith and kin. In our modern culture, human beings have become too utilitarian, and utilitarianism is a rajasic quality. We think primarily in terms of things that are useful to us. So we take care of trees because they give us fruit, wood, oxygen, and many other good things. But even when we do take care of the trees we do so as part of the mutuality of interest between humans and trees. This is good, but we can take a step further and say that we take care of trees, not just because they are useful to us, but because of their intrinsic spiritual value; they have a right to be what they are. Our idea of usefulness is also very narrow and short-term. Because of such short-term views we have allowed the destruction of forests on a large scale. We concern ourselves with human rights, but we also need to be concerned with nature's rights, with the rights of trees. This is the fundamental shift we need; we need to shift from a utilitarian to a spiritual worldview; from a rajasic to a sattvic quality.

We may look after our trees because they are useful to us, but we also need to respect them, pay homage to them and love them as we love a neighbour, because trees are our neighbours too. We should not make judgements about them, saying that 'this tree is in my way or not useful,' or 'I can do without this tree.' Trees have a right to stand unpolluted, undisturbed, uncontaminated, uncut. Trees look after us, like a mother feeding a baby at her breast, a father working hard to look after his children, or friends and neighbours working to look after one another. We may have to take something from the tree—fruit or perhaps wood—but we take it as a gift to us, not as a right. If we cut down a tree to build a house, the tree's timber is a gift to us and we take it with deep gratitude.

JUST IMAGINE THAT the seed we plant already has everything in it: a mighty oak is encapsulated in one little acorn. However complex the microchips we produce for our computers, they cannot compete with the complexity of an acorn. In a little acorn there is enshrined more information, more history and memory than in a microchip! And so you plant the acorn. It has to be planted in soil. You cannot just put it on the shelf and say, 'What a wonderful oak you are.' No, you have to allow it to germinate in the damp, dark soil. And out of that one acorn grows a tree that will last for hundreds of years, producing thousand of new acorns, year after year. That is the economy, spirituality and sustainability of nature. We humans, conditioned by rajasic culture, make something today, use it tomorrow, and throw it away the day after, filling up our landfill sites. And we call that 'human ingenuity'! We know nothing about sustainability in comparison to the mighty oak tree and its acorns.

We may talk about human justice. But what about Earth justice? Very few of us are prepared to stand up for trees and say 'I will fight for the rights of this tree.' Yet with a selfish, narrow-minded attitude we cut down our forests, and no one is there to speak for the trees. Lawyers will defend anyone who asks, but trees cannot ask for defence. Clearly, we need a new jurisprudence as a basis for our constitutions. The United Nations needs a new legal instrument to enable lawyers to defend forests, because they too have a right to live without being damaged. When human rights are given higher status over the rights of trees and the rights of nature, then they become rajasic rights. The sattvic quality requires the recognition that all living beings have an intrinsic right to live.

We seem to think, with our rajasic mindset, that nature is a mere resource for us to use as we please. But nature is not just a resource; it has its own reason to exist. The idea that human beings are in charge of the Earth, that we are the master species, is not a sattvic outlook. Every species has its rightful place in the scheme of things. All species have the right to live in their own way. We are not the masters, we are not in charge, we are not even managers or stewards ('steward' implies a touch of superiority); we are simply friends of the Earth. And 'friend' is a very beautiful word, because as friends we do not have expectations of one another. Unconditional friendship means you respect the person, love and accept him or her as he or she is, and therefore, if we are friends of the Earth and friends of the trees, then we respect them as our friends. Friendship is a supreme sattvic quality.

An ecological legal system would be a practical way to move forward, but it is our attitude to nature that requires a real transformation. Our attitude seems to be that the human species can be supported at the expense of all other species, and that resources like soil, air, water, trees, rivers, mountains—everything—are there for us to do what we like with as long as it benefits the human race. This rajasic attitude has to change. Unless we fundamentally change our view of the world, planting a few trees here and there is simply not going to be enough. Although planting trees always appears to be a good sattvic practice, it has to be more than a commercial activity for it to be considered truly sattvic. When the mind is embedded in sattvic motivation, only then is a physical action truly transformed into a sattvic action; the inner and the outer need to cohere for the sattvic to emerge.

The Buddha was enlightened when sitting under a tree. This was when he saw the interconnectedness of all life. He saw the clouds gathering and bringing water to the tree. He saw birds sitting in the tree, the leaves falling from the tree and the worms eating them and putting goodness back into the soil. The nutrients in the soil and the water from the clouds were helping to feed the tree. Sitting under the tree he witnessed the whole cycle of life and saw that all is connected, all is interdependent. There is no separate existence of any particular item, no separate soul, no separate entity; we are all connected. This realisation enlightened and enchanted him.

There is no great magic about the idea of spiritual enlightenment: the insight that I am not separate from you, a tree is not separate from me, blacks are not separate from whites, Muslims from Christians. The idea of separation is ignorance. And the idea of relatedness and oneness is enlightenment. The moment you see the interconnectedness, the unity of life, you are enlightened.

The tree has a spiritual meaning in every religious and cultural tradition. The tree of life and the tree of knowledge are universal metaphors. We have to listen to the speaking tree. Trees are central to our lives, but many still think that they are inferior and human beings superior.

We need to abandon the arrogant thought that humans are a superior species. We need to acknowledge that all living things depend on each other. This is the true meaning of the word 'sacred'; it means that life exists through sacrifice. When a father or mother helps a child, it is done with love, without self-consciousness. This is true sacrifice. It is the same when trees sacrifice their fruit to feed us, and their leaves to feed the earth and the worms to make the soil fertile. Sacrifice need not involve hardship. Sacrifice is an expression of love, of mutuality and of generosity. To receive this gift with gratitude is sacred. Life gives life to maintain life. We humans need not be the parasites of the Earth. Instead, we are part of the web of life. This sense of the sacred is the source of ecological humility.

My mother loved bees. Her ecological humility was evident when she said, "Bees are the greatest teachers, even greater teachers than the Buddha." And that is saying something, because the Buddha was supposed to be the greatest teacher in India.

According to my mother, if you want to learn the lessons of transformation you can learn from the honeybee. What does the honeybee do? It goes from flower to flower collecting a little nectar here and a little nectar there, never too much. And what do we humans do? We dig up minerals or extract oil and we take, take and take until there is nothing left. Honeybees never do that; they just take what they need.

What do they do with the nectar they take? They transform it into sweet, delicious, healing honey. If we could take something from nature and transform it into something good, like great artists, this would be an example of sattvic practice. We could say then that humans have eco-intelligence, that they have spirituality and generosity. But we seem to be the greatest waste-makers upon Earth; we are filling landfills with our waste. Waste is tamasic, and a sin against nature. In nature there is no waste; even those apples that are not eaten by humans, birds or wasps fall back to the soil and become compost, which nourishes the earth. That is the beauty of nature. While honeybees are taking nectar from the flowers, they pollinate them; they are true networkers and master matchmakers, as well as teachers of transformation.

Honeybees are an example of natural spirituality. They seem to know and practise the cyclical pattern of nature—everything comes from nature and returns to nature—whereas humans have invented a linear way: take, use and throw away. The cyclical way is the sattvic way, and the linear way of industrial pollution, depletion and waste, designed by civilisation, is the tamasic way.

Over the past 300 years industrial society has, knowingly or unknowingly, built rajasic and tamasic infrastructures. Now we are facing dissatisfaction, anguish and confusion. This is the time of transformation.

Sattvic Identity: From 'me' to 'we'

THIS TRANSFORMATION HAS to be a transformation in our consciousness and a movement away from our separational, rajasic or tamasic identity to our shared, sattvic, relational identity.

René Descartes, the 17th-century French philosopher, was the father of dualistic philosophy and science. He said, "I think, therefore I am." *Cogito ergo sum*. That was one of the starting points of the separational identity. Nature is out there, separate from humans. An alternative identity is 'You are, therefore I am.' It is a relational and holistic identity—earth, air, fire, water and food are, so therefore I am. My parents, my ancestors are, therefore I am.

Who am I? Am I just an Indian, a writer, a man? What is my true identity?

I am made of the entire evolution of the Earth; I am a microcosm of the macrocosm. There is nothing in the universe which is not in me. The entire universe is encapsulated in me, as a tree is encapsulated in a seed. There is nothing out there in the universe which is not here, in me. Earth, air, fire, water, time, space, light, history, evolution and consciousness—everything is in me. At the first moment of the Big Bang I was there, so I carry the entire evolution of the Earth in me. I also carry the billions of years of evolution to come. I am the past and the future. Our identity cannot be defined as narrowly as stating that I am British, Indian, Christian, Muslim, Hindu, Buddhist, a doctor or a lawyer. These rajasic identities are secondary, for convenience. Our sattvic or true identity is universal, cosmic. When I become aware of this primal, sattvic identity I can then see my true place in the universe, my every action becomes a sattvic action, a spiritual action.

When I am a gardener, with my transformed consciousness, I am manifesting the beauty, the enormity, the continuity and the abundance of the universe. And like the honeybee, I am transforming something which was just inedible seed into fruit. Fruit is honey! When a bee makes honey, I make fruit. Every one of us has that possibility, that imagination, and that creativity for transformation which our industrialised and economic systems have weakened and in some cases destroyed. If I want to awaken that creativity, that imagination, that human spirit, then I have to become a transformer: wheat into bread, clay into sculptures, words into poems, paper into pictures. I have to transform myself from being a consumer to a maker and bring joy into everything I make.

Joy is the most fundamental sattvic quality. In India the word for joy is *ananda*. When you become a Hindu monk you are given a new name which always ends in *ananda*: Yogananda, Muktananda, Shivananda. Why Yogananda? Why does *ananda* have to be added to Yoga? You may be doing yoga every day—morning, evening, day after day, but still be miserable. What is the use of doing yoga like that? So yoga must be accompanied by *ananda*—joy. The same goes for gardening, farming, baking, even washing dishes—whatever you are doing, do it with joy, with pleasure, with love and creativity. It is hard to be a good painter if you do not enjoy painting, a good poet if you do not enjoy writing, a good baker if you do not enjoy cooking. The baking of bread is a poem; the growing of flowers and vegetables is a painting. We need to transform our day-to-day work into a work of art and a work of spirit. This is called sattvic work.

Ananda Coomaraswamy said, "An artist is not a special kind of person, but every person is a special kind of artist." The industrial system of mass production takes away our unique artistry. So in our daily lives we need to transform our work into sattvic work—work as poetry and poetry as work.

Tamasic Consumerism

The lack of imagination in everyday life has created a vacuum which is filled by the tamasic quality of extreme consumerism, and in turn such tamasic consumerism fuels global warming.

Whatever we consume—foods, clothes, housing, agriculture, transport, technology, holidays—much of it is mass produced and is dependent on the use of fossil fuel on a massive scale. Yet higher living standards, higher economic growth and higher consumption have been and still continue to be the unchallenged aspiration of all governments and all industrial societies.

However, the challenge of global warming is slowly bringing about a certain shift in the consciousness of politicians, policy makers and business leaders. Even the mainstream media and conservative think-tanks are beginning to talk about economies as subordinate to ecology. More and more people are realising that we cannot go on as before: business as usual is no longer an option, because our non-stop consumerism is not sustainable.

At present, this shift in consciousness is only skin deep. The high level of carbon emissions we are producing is merely the symptom of the problem, not the root cause. To treat the symptom, policy makers are looking at bio-fuels instead of fossil fuels. They are looking to find new sources of energy, such as solar, wind and nuclear power. Their deep desire is to go on consuming as much as they have been, perhaps even more, but only through so-called sustainable sources. Are we not deluding ourselves in thinking that consumerism and sustainability can go hand in hand? Is this not a case of having your cake and eating it?

The climate crisis is actually the crisis of consumerism. Whether we actually need more clothes, more computers or more cosmetics, is seen as irrelevant. The problem is that we have to have them; we have to keep consuming in order to keep the wheels of the economy turning; we have to keep buying to keep people in employment, no matter what the consequences. More than three-quarters of the world's forests have already been cleared to feed our consumerism, and still there is no halt. Every year a further area of virgin forests the size of Austria is cleared from the Amazon to Indonesia, so that we can keep consuming. We go to war to secure oil supplies, so that we can keep consuming. And now we merely wish to find some new miracle technology to avoid the consequence of our blind consumerism. But there is no such thing as consequence-free consumerism. We cannot escape the effects of our consumerist culture.

So the solution is not just to replace fossil fuels with bio-fuels, but to replace our quantitative consumerism with a qualitative lifestyle. We need to move away from more and global to less and local, from acquisitiveness to frugality, from accumulation to enjoyment, from employment to livelihood, and from desire to delight; in other words, from tamasic to sattvic and from materialism to spirituality. Rather than the consumption of natural resources, we need a culture of appreciation of the natural world.

A tsunami of consumerism is sweeping the world. Mild consumerism is rajasic, and could be manageable. But the present extreme form of consumerism is tamasic and it is bringing the Earth and humanity on a collision course. Humanity is so ruined by tamasic consumerism that even though we know that it is catastrophic, we are unable to change our course. Collectively, modern humanity does not know how to change course, and how to prevent the global juggernaut of consumerist culture from falling into an abyss.

Ownership is Rajasic, and Relationship is Sattvic

> "In the days of the white settlement, the natives of North America found ownership of land an incomprehensible concept. And so they lost it when the Europeans made them sign pieces of paper that were equally incomprehensible to them. They felt they belonged to the land, but the land did not belong to them."
>
> *Eckhart Tolle*

IN NATIVE, INDIGENOUS CULTURES there was no notion of ownership. Those 'primitive' peoples did not consider themselves as owners of nature. As tigers, elephants, horses, birds and other species were fed, watered and sheltered without owning the land or the forest, so were the American Indians, the bush people of the Kalahari, the

Adivasis of India and the Aboriginals of Australia. They flourished for thousands of years without owning the earth. The American Indians believed that the present generation holds the land in trust for future generations. Therefore, before we act, we must think: what will be the impact of our action on the seventh generation after us?

The idea of owning land and animals began with the development of agriculture and so-called civilisation. But in earlier times, the practice of ownership was not so damaging. People worked with hand tools, cultivated the land within walking distance, and fished the oceans with small boats and small fishing nets. For them, nature was not a commodity; rather it was a partner in pursuit of livelihood. With such a benign mindset and low-impact technology, ownership did not cause huge problems.

But now, with advanced technology, mass production, global commerce, speedy communication and an unquenchable thirst and rajasic desire for fame, fortune and power, the concept of ownership has a devastating impact on the survival of the Earth itself.

In this context it is right to be questioning the very notion of ownership of nature. We are part of the web of life, not the owners, nor even the managers or the stewards, of the Earth. Instead we should consider ourselves to be friends or trustees of the Earth; ownership is rajasic, and trusteeship is sattvic.

The idea of trusteeship, in our time, was formulated by Mahatma Gandhi. He believed that every generation of humans should assume responsibility on behalf of all living beings and on behalf of the future generations as trustees. It is the responsibility of a good trustee not to squander the original capital—only the interest or the income should be spent. Trustees are not allowed, by law, to use the money for their own personal advantage. They can receive expenses; which means that they can take what they really need but no more. Trustees must use the income of the trust for the benefit of the general public.

In the capitalist system, it is assumed that natural resources are revenue rather than capital. The fact that we call them 'resources' shows that we consider them objects to be owned and used. But

Gandhi believed that the Earth itself is capital, and we are not to deplete it. As trustees, we need to look for ways to replenish and enhance rather than diminish the assets of the Earth. Only the renewable fruit of the Earth can be shared among people and other creatures. All living creatures can of course enjoy the apples from the tree, but not destroy the tree itself. If we have to cut down trees, then as trustees it is our responsibility to plant even greater numbers than we have cut down. The fruits of the trees, forests, rivers, mountains and all other natural resources are there to be shared for the continuation of life. All creatures, humans and non-humans, should have access to the fruits of the Earth, rather than a small number of people own the natural capital and exclude the others from it, which leads to the tamasic consequences of violent revolutions and wars.

This radical shift in our consciousness need not preclude entrepreneurship or imaginative new ventures, but such ventures should be motivated by self-enrichment and self-seeking; rather they should be motivated by the sattvic desire to serve and replenish the earth. To establish the notion of trusteeship, we have to begin with a change of heart and a transformation of our worldview.

If we continue to charge along the path of ownership and hope that all people—six billion of us—can have access to the same kind of resources, we will soon be disappointed. So we need to develop a new worldview which is different from the rajasic ideology of high living standards for everyone through the spread of ownership. The rajasic eye sees nature as property; the sattvic eye sees nature as a gift. In the sattvic worldview, quality of life is more important than quantity of possessions.

Is there a relationship between people suffering from chronic poverty on the one hand, and ownership of natural resources by the few on the other? The answer is yes. The majority of urban slum dwellers and the rural poor have no direct access to land, forests, or fishing. These natural resources are vested in a few private hands. The ownership of the means of livelihood has become more and more concentrated.

How can we own the land, forests, rivers and oceans? Like air and sunshine, food and water are the gifts of nature—and should be equally accessible to all.

According to some biologists, there are about 300 million species upon this Earth. Apart from humans, all other creatures—lions, elephants, monkeys, snakes, bees, worms or butterflies—have access to free food and water. Only human beings are deprived of free food and water, the basic necessities of survival. We have created a rajasic system of ownership which puts humans below all other species as far as access to food and water is concerned. There may be mountains of food rotting in warehouses, and crops of grain burned to maintain the market price, but if humans have no money, they can have neither food nor water.

We have built a rajasic system which turns food and water into commodities to be bought and sold with money which is controlled by moneylenders and banks. Money is supposed to be a medium of exchange, but in reality it has become the ruler of our lives. And as money is always kept in short supply, there is no way all human beings can be guaranteed to have enough and therefore no guaranteed provision of food and water for every human being upon the Earth.

So poverty is not a natural phenomenon, it is a result of rajasic turning into tamasic design.

Now, fighting poverty has itself become big business. It has become a source of making money by those who already have plenty of it. For the past sixty years, government after government of every country has spoken about reducing poverty. UN agencies, aid agencies, the World Trade Organisation, the World Bank, the International Monetary Fund and charitable organisations have all been busy with the business of eliminating poverty. World leaders have been designing Millennium Development Goals with the best of intentions. But in spite of all the rhetoric and media hype, and the slogans of 'making poverty history', the poverty of the poor continues to deepen as the wealth of the wealthy continues to rise. The net flow of wealth is constantly flowing from the poor to the rich countries.

So the urgent challenge facing the world is not to give more *to* the poor, but to take less *from* the poor; to get off their backs and get out of their way so that they can look after themselves.

The beneficiaries of poverty alleviation programmes have been contractors, engineers, planners, traders, government bureaucrats and aid officials. In the name of fighting poverty, big dams have been built, displacing communities and villages, forcing millions of people away from their homes and into city slums. In the name of increasing food production, agriculture has been industrialised and mechanised, making farm labourers redundant, family farms bankrupt and small farms indebted and uneconomic. In the name of increasing employment, mass production of consumer goods has been introduced, making artisans and craftspeople jobless. To put it simply, most efforts to defeat poverty have succeeded in increasing it—benefiting the privileged and the powerful.

Poverty will never be eliminated unless we eliminate injustice. Free access to natural resources to obtain food and water is the natural right of all living beings. Denial of that right is the cause of poverty. Poverty is not the problem; injustice is the problem. Wealth is the problem. In order to 'make poverty history' we have to make wealth history.

We need to make a fundamental shift, a paradigm shift, a shift from ownership to relationship. We do not own nature, we have a relationship with nature. Nature does not belong to us, we belong to nature. Nature is a gift to nourish all living beings. Ownership imprisons us in materialism. Relationships liberate and lead us to spiritual and physical wellbeing.

The end of private ownership does not mean the establishment of state ownership or collective ownership. The problem is not whether nature is owned by private individuals or governments. The problem is with the concept of ownership itself. The fault lies in the idea that humans can own and possess nature. Ownership means control, relationship means partnership and participation. We cannot control nature but we can participate in the process of nature. We humans are nature too. Whatever is born is nature. Mothers take pre-natal and post-natal care; natal, native and nature come from the same root.

Poverty is not caused by lack of food, it is caused by lack of access to food. There is abundance in nature. One apple seed produces hundreds of apples, year after year, for many years. If millions of species can satisfy their hunger and thirst without money, why can humans not do the same? The problem is not poverty—poverty is the result of seizure of the gifts of the Earth by the few.

An Eleven-Point Programme for Sattvic Action

IT IS EASY TO feel impotent in the shadow of the political, consumerist and corporate interests that exercise so much rajasic power over our lives and the environment. Questions instinctively arise when we feel a sense of urgency about the predicament of the natural world: 'What can I do?' 'How can I effect change?' 'How can I make my voice heard?' 'How can I live a sattvic life?'

Mahatma Gandhi's answer was very simple and straightforward: "Be the change you want to see in the world." Political and corporate change will remain superficial and inadequate without personal change. Indeed, without individual action these larger changes will not occur. Political change will only happen when large numbers of people practise what they believe. When there is a big enough groundswell of opinion and enough action at the grassroots, then governments will be forced to bring in laws and create structural transformations. We have to make the bottom-up changes in order to force top-down transformation.

Here is my eleven-point programme for sattvic action. Each and every one of us can start to live sattvic values in our everyday life. We can all take these few simple steps to combat the rajasic values of consumerism, address the problem of global warming and begin to live a joyful life.

1. Change our attitudes

Our industrial culture is human-centred and utilitarian. We value nature because of its usefulness. If we want a sustainable future, we need to change this mindset. We need to recognise that all life has intrinsic value. Without such a shift in our personal attitudes towards the natural world, a sustainable sattvic lifestyle cannot be achieved. In place of the utilitarian calculus, a reverential, respectful worldview is required. Then we will destroy less, poison less, kill less, protect more, respect more and celebrate more.

2. Live simply

A high living standard—measured by money and material acquisition—has become the be-all and end-all of modern society. For an eco-friendly life we need to seek quality of life instead. More bluntly, we need to live more simply, so that others may simply live. Any fool can make life complicated; it requires genius to make it simple.

3. Consume less

Fifty years ago the world's population was 3 billion. Now it has doubled to 6 billion and humans, at their present rate of consumption, are exceeding the capacity of the Earth—something for which we all have to take personal responsibility. Someone living in the West consumes fifty times more than a person in the Third World; this effectively means that the Western population is multiplied fifty times. Therefore, live more lightly, taking from nature only what is needed, so as to make a smaller footprint on the Earth. "There is enough in the world for everybody's need, but not enough for anybody's greed," said Mahatma Gandhi.

4. Waste not

Waste is a sin against nature, a curse of modern life and a tamasic quality of the highest order. Every day millions of tons of waste are thrown into the natural world, which it simply cannot cope with. The pile of old cookers, washing machines, fridges, computers and televisions is now accumulating at six million tons a year, a rate that is expected to double by 2010, and most of it ends up in landfill, wasting resources and posing risks to health and the environment. Millions of plastic bottles and plastic bags are cluttering and clogging the system, polluting rivers and oceans. Therefore, reusing, mending and recycling must be regarded as great sattvic virtues. One very simple step is to reuse plastic bags, or to take a cloth bag when you go shopping. Another is to rediscover the old maxim, 'make do and mend', to resist the temptation to replace utensils (old cookers and machines) and furniture when the old ones will do. In doing this, we will strike at consumerism.

5. Use no harmful products

When cleaning the house and washing clothes, use environmentally friendly and organic products. In building, clothing and furnishing. give preference to natural and locally sourced materials.

6. Walk

Our lives have become dependent on cars, even for short distances. This lack of exercise makes us obese and unhealthy. We live in homes, drive around in machines and work in offices; we hardly ever come into contact with the natural world. But if we do not know, see and experience nature, how can we love her? And if we do not love nature, how can we protect her? So walking in nature, taking walking holidays and walking to work can be a real doorway to sattvic living.

7. Bake bread

Gandhi advocated spinning and weaving cloth at home as a way of defying consumerism, reconnecting us with tradition and proclaiming the virtues of simplicity. For us, making our own bread can serve the same purpose.

8. Meditate

Our lives have become too busy and stressful. The pressure of work, the pressure to succeed, to achieve, to cope with excess information—all this increases our stress levels. To restore the balance, we need to take some time during the day for personal replenishment, for the development of the soul, for reflection, for creativity, and for our proper relationship with the natural world to develop and grow. Every day, for at least half an hour, we need solitude, stillness and silence, so that the rest of the day is built on a foundation of sattvic tranquillity.

9. Work less

In spite of mass production, industrialisation, automation and mechanisation, we are overworked, often to the point of exhaustion. Too often by the time people come home from work they have no energy to do anything other than sit in front of the television. In spite of our wealth and unprecedented economic growth, our work makes us slaves. For a sustainable future we need to work less, do less, spend less and be more. Slow down and go further. From simply being will emerge relationships, celebrations and joy. Sustainable living is joyful living. The current system of debt, mortgage payments and other obligations forces us to work more, but if we were conscious, we could redesign our lives to create a better work/life balance. Where there is a will there is a way!

10. Be informed

No one can lay down a blueprint for sattvic living; each of us has to develop our own ideas. But we have to build on all the new thinking in this field. There are books, magazines and courses which can help us. We need to make time to study.

11. Organise

Vested interests will always find ways to fool people and to seek profit and power which damage the Earth. Therefore we need to be awake and alert and speak out against the exploitative actions of the powerful—speak truth to power! But such protests cannot be made alone; we have to be in solidarity with organisations working for a sustainable future. Choose an organisation which suits your temperament and work within your local community. Form a local group and take an interest in local politics, organise, communicate and share your concerns with others.

The Paradox of Our Age

We have bigger houses but smaller families;
more conveniences, but less time.
We have more degrees, but less sense;
more knowledge, but less judgement;
more medicines, but less healthiness.
We've been all the way to the Moon and back,
but we have trouble crossing the street to meet the
  new neighbours.
We have built more computers to hold more
  information,
to produce more copies than ever,
but we have less communication.
We have become long on quantity,
but short on quality.
These are the times of fast foods but slow digestion;
tall man but short character;
steep profits but shallow relationships.
It is a time when there is much in the window,
but nothing in the room.

His Holiness the 14th Dalai Lama

Chapter Four

SATTVIC ECOLOGY

Green Spirit

Dissolve rajasic pride with sattvic humility.
Dissolve rajasic greed with sattvic generosity.
Dissolve rajasic arrogance with sattvic gratitude.
Dissolve tamasic anger with sattvic kindness.
Dissolve tamasic ignorance with sattvic awareness.

HOW THE THREE QUALITIES, sattva, rajas and tamas, relate to the ecology movement has been a constant question in my mind. I do think that there are three ways to understand and practise ecology. A reverential attitude to nature is sattvic ecology. A scientific and analytical understanding of nature is rajasic ecology, and a utilitarian, tamasic relationship with nature can no longer be called ecology; it is a kind of exploitative environmentalism.

Sattvic ecology needs to be enriched with a spiritual understanding of the links between humans and the millions of other forms of life.

Given the fullness of the environmentalist agenda, it is surprising that many modern approaches to nature are one-dimensional. They are purely scientific, and as a result they are rajasic. They lack depth and wholeness. Scientific environmentalism started with the publication of *Silent Spring* in 1962. The Club of Rome report, *The Limits to Growth* (1972), added impetus. *Blueprint for Survival* by *The Ecologist* magazine continued the momentum. And the 1972 UN conference on the environment in Stockholm became a landmark event. All these important milestones have contributed greatly to building today's environmental movement. Governments, the media, the scientific community and a large number of non-governmental organisations and professional environmentalists seem to think that they can treat the symptoms of environmental crisis, control pollution, conserve resources and manage nature better for long-term human benefit. The Norwegian philosopher Arne Naess has called this "shallow ecology". I could call it rajasic ecology.

Less recognised but running parallel to scientific environmentalism has been a search for spiritual ecology. A small number of people started to look at the more fundamental causes of the environmental crisis in the mid-1960s, and questioned the values and culture which gave birth to the desire for unlimited economic growth and unquestioning consumerism. E. F. Schumacher gave voice to this approach in his classic essay, 'Buddhist Economics'. He was perhaps the only eminent Western economist who would have dared to put those two words together. He was a holistic ecologist.

In line with Schumacher, in the 1970s Ivan Illich also contributed to the school of thought which based economics and ecology on ethical and sattvic foundations. Both Schumacher and Illich derived much inspiration from the thought of Mahatma Gandhi, from Buddhism, and from other Eastern and Western spiritual traditions.

It was pointed out that the scientific view of environmentalism is based on the separation of subject from object—the observer from the observed—whereas sattvic ecology sees a seamless continuum between the observer and the observed. The scientific environmentalists talk about nature out there, whereas for the sattvic ecologist there is no separation between nature and humanity. There is no such thing as the environment out there, of which humans are in charge. We are part and parcel of the environment. It is a case of understanding the relationship between innumerable life forms, of which human life is one.

One common emotion among the scientists seems to be the driving force behind the widespread concern for the health of our fragile planet: fear. They fear the consequences of climate change. They fear the melting ice caps and rising sea levels, which will overwhelm low-lying countries such as Bangladesh and bring catastrophe to cities such as London. They fear that pesticides and other chemical residues in our food may damage our health and the health of our children. They fear the depletion of energy sources—the lights in our homes will go out. They fear that we may already be reaching a tipping point beyond which natural systems are irrecoverably damaged and civilisation will collapse.

Fear may be a useful defence mechanism to make people act to protect the environment. Fear of the end of civilisation can motivate people to change policies and lifestyles, to make the difficult cuts in carbon emissions which are necessary to combat global warming. Fear has a place, but it must be kept strictly in its place. Fear is a tamasic quality; if we allow it to overwhelm us, to rule us, if fear becomes the driving force behind our environmentalism, then we are likely to be debilitated, disempowered and depressed.

We need to remember that the power of love is greater than the power of fear. Our lives and our actions need to be rooted in love of the Earth and of the natural world. Most people have an intuitive love of nature; walking in wild woods, swimming in clean rivers and caring for animals is as natural to us as looking after our children and our families. Most of us are intuitively friends of the Earth, even if we do not know it. For the majority of people in the world, caring for the Earth is a way of life rather than a way of crisis management.

The health of the Earth is as much a moral and spiritual challenge as it is a political and economic one. Solutions founded in fear will be wrong solutions, panic reactions to a particular crisis. Because of fear, we build nuclear weapons. Then to save ourselves from them, we build nuclear bunkers. Because of fear of scarcity, we pursue economic growth and globalisation, transporting goods around the world, using fossil fuels which cause global warming. To save ourselves from global warming we want to cover the Earth with windmills, nuclear power stations or large-scale production of bio-fuels, which takes land out of food production and causes food scarcity. A vicious cycle of fear develops. In the past, we were told: 'Be good or you will go to hell.' Now we are told: 'Recycle, or civilisation will come to an end!'

Fear is a poor reason for being an environmentalist. Sattvic ecology provides a more profound and solid reason for our environmentalism: a conviction that the Earth is our only home, and living in harmony with her is good and sufficient in itself. A simple and sattvic way of life, respecting the intrinsic value of all living beings—humans and other than humans—is the proper way of life. Global warming or no global warming, caring for the Earth is our spiritual obligation.

Some Christians have found it difficult to embrace this sattvic ecology because *Genesis* speaks of human beings having dominion over nature: God created the world and made humankind its guardian. Many scientists who practised Christianity in their private lives unwittingly transferred the idea to science and went out to steal the secrets of nature for the benefit of humankind. But there are other Christian traditions. For example that of St Francis, who is the patron saint of sattvic ecology. He did not talk about animals, but he talked with them. He understood the spirit of wolves and birds. For him, the sun was his brother, the moon his sister and the entire universe one family. If God is divine, his creation has to be divine too. There can be no greater sin than polluting and misusing nature, which is a gift from God to all his creatures. This awareness is found in the Celtic tradition of Christianity and in the writings of Hildegard of Bingen.

For the Hindus, God is not outside nature. The universe is a dance of Shiva. As the dance and the dancer cannot be separated, the creator cannot be separated from the creation. Every blade of grass, every drop of water, every breath of wind and every flame of fire is imbibed with the sacred. In fact the universe and God are one and the same thing; there is no dualism, God is not a person somewhere in heaven controlling the world.

In the Hindu view of the world, everything is sacred: Earth is sacred, water is sacred, air and fire are sacred, and space and time are sacred. Because nature is sacred, it is good in itself. We may not manipulate or pollute it, exploit or deplete it. This is the principle of *ahimsa*, non-violence towards nature. As humans cannot create life, they have no right to destroy it. This is the attitude of reverence as Albert Schweitzer put it—reverence for life.

The utilitarian view of tamasic environmentalism believes that nature is there for human exploitation. Nature has an economic purpose; therefore she must be managed, owned and used.

Sattvic ecologists recognise the intrinsic value of nature. They talk about paying attention to quality over quantity. They teach people to become aware of when enough is enough. The Taoist master, Lao Tzu, said that when you know how much is enough, you will realise that you already have enough. But when you do not know how much is enough, then however much you have you will never have enough. The definition of being rich is not that you possess vast quantities of objects and goods, but rather you are rich when you know that you do not need any more. This wisdom to differentiate between greed and need stems from a sattvic outlook.

Simple living and high thinking were among the teachings of the Sufi poet Rumi, who sang the glory of divine abundance and yet rejoiced in the gift of contentment. If we read the poetry of Rumi in an ecological context, he is another patron saint of ecology, like St Francis.

The Jewish tradition points in the same direction when it says, 'Give me neither poverty nor riches', because material acquisition is the mother of poverty, and when one is able to live in the heaven of contentment, the hell of poverty and greed vanishes instantly.

All the spiritual traditions work at a psychological level to promote the sattvic ecology of relationship with oneself, with fellow humans and with nature at large. When we are able to come to terms with our own soul and be at ease with our inner consciousness, we will be able to develop a sattvic worldview.

But rajasic environmentalists argue that time is running out; we cannot afford the luxury of bringing about an inner transformation of consciousness. The path of spiritual and sattvic ecology is too slow. Immediate action by governments to implement laws to protect the environment is urgently needed. This sense of urgency and impatience ignores the fact that in the last thirty or so years governments have enacted many environmental laws and environmentalists have produced thousands of books analysing the urgency of the environmental predicament and forecasting doom and collapse, yet they have not been able to stem the tide of economic globalisation, population explosion, or the destruction of ecosystems and biodiversity. Now is the time to look at the big picture with a long-term view, and develop sattvic ecology.

One important source of sattvic ecology is found in the cultures of native peoples around the world. The scientific civilisation of Europe has tended to consider the traditions of tribal peoples as savage, backward, undeveloped and inferior. This is a fundamental folly of the modern mind. Although traditional societies such as those in Australia, the Americas, Africa and Asia collapsed because of invasion by rajasic and tamasic forces, they lived in harmony with nature in a sustainable manner for tens of thousands of years.

A sense of beauty, wilderness, unity and interdependence is deeply embedded in the wisdom of traditional societies. The native peoples of North America considered the Earth as their grandmother and the sky as their grandfather.

The Aboriginal peoples of Australia saw human existence rooted in dreamtime, with no beginning and no end. Dreamtime is the creation itself. It is not linear time, it is cyclical. Everything moves in cycles, everything returns. Rajasic environmentalists think in terms of evolution, development and progress. All these concepts are linear. Cyclical is sattvic. The linear view of the world looks at the past as unevolved, undeveloped and inferior. This will not help us to move out of our ecological impasse. We need to find some other philosophical tools, and we can find them in the cultures of native peoples.

In industrial societies, beneath the surface of people's lives there lies a state of confusion and fear. People find themselves walking on a treadmill. The economy is booming, yet there is little contentment or satisfaction. Highways are filled with cars, but people feel they are getting nowhere. They have everything, yet they feel they have nothing. The Jeffersonian ideal of the pursuit of happiness is proving to be an endless quest, and its attainment is still a mirage.

On the one hand, people are driven to all kinds of desperate rajasic and tamasic acts; cults, sects, virtual reality, drugs and umpteen other forms of escapism are attracting people to abandon their everyday lives, which are often empty of meaning and without a sense of belonging. On the other hand, there is a growing quest for sattvic values to find fulfilment in a deeper relationship with nature. Some people are returning to work the land and grow organic food. They are developing a sense of community within their neighbourhood. They are recreating a sense of place and a sense of home. Instead of flying to the Bahamas for rajasic holidays, people are walking the coastal paths or the wild moors in their own country.

Sattvic ecology must emerge from the fringes. The Eco-Village Network, the New Economics, Moral Economy and Community Supported Agriculture, Deep Ecology and Gaia—all are expressions of an emerging spirituality which is embedded in interconnected sattvic systems.

We do not have to go to a church, a temple or a mosque to practise sattvic ecology. When we look at the world with the eyes of the heart, rivers and mountains become our mosques, forests and fields become our synagogues, trees become our temples, celebration of the seasons becomes the communion and appreciation of beauty becomes the prayer. Thus sattvic ecology is a way of re-enchanting everyday life in its luminous simplicity.

The Point of Return

PEOPLE OFTEN ASK ME, "Are you a pessimist or an optimist?" My answer is, "I am an optimist", because pessimism is tamasic. I know that at the moment pessimism is in fashion. Scientists, environmentalists and climatologists are claiming that collapse is around the corner and civilisation is coming to an end. Book after book tells us that we have passed the tipping point and have reached the point of no return. The skies are saturated with carbon dioxide and the atmosphere is filled with greenhouse gases. We are told over and over that whatever we do, we cannot reverse the rise in temperature or prevent the sea from flooding London! What happened to New Orleans will happen to New York. Global warming is here to stay. The scenario of doom and gloom is expounded by experts and activists alike.

I do not underestimate the severity of the climate crisis. I respect the scientists who are predicting a catastrophic future for humanity. I agree that our present way of life, so dependent on the use of fossil fuel, is hanging on a cliff edge. If we go any further, we will fall into the abyss. So the only thing we can do now is to take a step back; I call it 'the point of return'. We need to return to a way of life which is free from damaging dependence on fossil fuel. At present we burn millions of barrels of petroleum every day for our food, clothes, homes, heating, lighting, transport and entertainment. This way of life is not only wasteful and unsustainable; it is also very dangerous. It took nature 200 million years to create the vast store of fossil energy which we have almost spent in 200 years. The speed with which we are exhausting fossil energy is incredible.

Civilisation is collectively passing through a dark night of the soul; it is passing through an ecological, social and spiritual crisis. At this moment it is easy to be a pessimist. It is easy to bury our heads in the sand and say that it is all too late; we have reached the point of no return, nothing can be done, we have run out of time. Such pessimism is born of fear.

Pessimism is tamasic because it is disempowering. How can we be sure that it is too late? Giving up is not an option. The challenges of global warming, global poverty and global greed are indeed serious. Now is the time to wake up and unite to use our collective wisdom, our creativity and ingenuity, our human imagination, to redesign our economic, political and social systems on sattvic principles to suit the needs of our time. This wasteful, destructive and consumerist tamasic culture is not God-given. It has only developed in the last 250 years or so, and in the context of the evolutionary timescale 250 years is a very short time. What was created by humans can be changed by humans. We are capable of moving from tamas to sattva; we can reconstruct our economy in harmony with ecology. We have to get to work with optimism: optimism is born of love. At this critical time we need to evoke our courage to love the Earth and be of service to the Earth and to her people. Optimism is empowering and inspiring; optimism is not necessarily wishful thinking. Optimism is the source of right action. Let us rise to the challenge. Pessimism is the refuge of cowards, while optimism is the source of courage. Pessimism breeds passivity; optimism leads to activism.

There is a word in Sanskrit for the point of return; it is *pratikraman*. Its opposite is *atikraman*, which means stepping outside our natural limits. *Atikraman* happens when we break the universal law. Returning to the centre of one's being or to the source of inner wisdom is *pratikraman*. These two Sanskrit words provide a useful handle to understanding the current human predicament and a possible way out. A profound introspection is needed to examine the state of our psyche; we need to ask, are we meeting our need or indulging our greed? Are we healing or wounding the Earth?

In the context of global warming, addiction to oil is *atikraman* and a return to the energy derived directly from air, water and sun is *pratikraman*. One way to begin our *pratikraman* is to stop and put a cap on the use of fossil fuels. We need a moratorium on the building of motorways and airport runways. No new homes should be built without insulation. We need to put an immediate freeze on industrial agriculture everywhere in the world. Once we have put a freeze on the use of fossil fuels then we can start the reduction process and the return journey to renewable resources. If we plan and manage our return journey carefully, we should be able to escape the projected meltdown. We were able to repair the hole in the ozone by reducing the use of CFCs, so we should be able to mitigate the extreme consequences of global warming if we can put an immediate cap on the use of fossil fuels now and prepare to make the return journey instantly.

To meet the challenge of global warming, we need to change from being consumers to being artists; we have to take refuge in the arts and crafts. As William Morris and Mahatma Gandhi advocated long ago, arts and crafts ignite our imagination, stimulate our creativity and bring us a sense of fulfilment. Poetry, painting, pottery, music, meditation, gardening, sculpting and other forms of arts and crafts can meet our basic human needs, producing beautiful objects to use which need not require the use of fossil fuels. Human happiness, true prosperity and joyful living can only emerge from a life of elegant simplicity.

We are at the point of return from the gross to the subtle, from the glamorous to the gracious, from hedonism to healing, from conquest of the earth to conservation of nature, and from quantities of possessions to quality of life. It is 'cool' to be an optimist.

Prayer for Peace

Lead me from death to life,
from falsehood to truth.

Lead me from despair to hope,
from fear to trust.

Lead me from hate to love,
from war to peace.

Let peace fill our hearts,
our world, our universe.

Peace, Peace, Peace!

Based on a Sanskrit mantra,
adapted by the author

Finding God

Sermons say read the Bible
To know God
Kneel and pray
To know God
Obey the Commandments
To know God
But yesterday
I saw a butterfly
Land on a withered leaf
Just before sunset
And at that moment
I knew God.

A Maori Meditation

Chapter Five

THREE KINDS OF DEVELOPMENT

Sattvic Development

The thought manifests as the word;
The word manifests as the deed;
The deed develops into habit;
And habit hardens into character.
So watch the thought and its ways with care,
And let it spring from love
Born out of concern for all beings.
The Buddha

DEVELOPMENT, AS COMMONLY understood, concerns economic, social and material wellbeing; it excludes the internal, personal and interpersonal wellbeing. But we need both. Without the external, there can be no internal, and vice versa. Sattvic development is holistic; it seeks economic and spiritual wellbeing simultaneously. What appear as opposites are in fact complementary. For the hungry, God manifests in bread, and for the overfed, in fasting. When there is a balance between fasting and feasting and when everyone is able to fast and feast, then spirituality and economic development reveal themselves as two sides of the same coin.

There are those who advocate economic wellbeing as the only goal of development. For them economic growth and rising living standards are ends in themselves; there is no other meaning to life than acquisition, possession and consumption; the Earth's resources are there to be owned and to be turned into usable goods. Nature is there to serve the economic needs of ever-growing human numbers. Economic development is the be-all and end-all of development.

Such exclusively economic and external development is rajasic.

Then there are those who believe they should keep their face towards God and their back towards the world. The world is full of sin, human birth itself is the mark of Original Sin, and human nature is intrinsically greedy, violent, competitive and aggressive. There is no redemption other than that offered by God on the Day of Judgement. In order to please God, they say it is necessary to renounce the material world and liberate oneself. Such denial of worldly existence is also rajasic.

This dichotomy between economic and spiritual development can be healed by cultivating a sense of the sattvic, which means a sense of balance and harmony between economic and spiritual needs.

Rajasic development has been tried by many. The World Bank, aid agencies, government departments, voluntary groups and individuals have been active in the field. More often than not these missionaries of materialism suffer from arrogance and prejudice: arrogance in the belief that the industrialised, urbanised, educated elite are already developed, and now the task is to spread this model to all corners of the world; and prejudice in the belief that tribal, rural, agrarian societies are undeveloped, and need secular schooling and modern medicine, computers and cameras, tractors and televisions. Without these mod cons, without roads and railways, without fridges and faxes, without cars and concrete buildings, without mobiles and iPods, their lives, to them, are primitive and poor.

With this rajasic arrogance and prejudice, governmental and non-governmental aid agencies have tried to lift the poor out of their misery and have failed. In the past fifty years the gap between the rich and the poor has widened as a consequence of rajasic developmental projects. Industrial modes of production have destroyed manual skills and cottage industries, big dams have displaced peasant populations. As a result, country people have been compelled to leave their rural dwellings and migrate to city slums. The chemicalised and mechanised monoculture of food production has pushed the agrarian labour force to seek their livelihood outside the agricultural sector, away from their communities and families. In short, rajasic development has failed in achieving even its own stated goals.

There have been a number of small-scale attempts at sattvic development, informed by spiritual values, but I would like to discuss just five.

Mahatma Gandhi and his vision of Sattvic Development as Service

Mahatma Gandhi in India was one of the early pioneers of sattvic development. He, with his wife and colleagues, went to live in a rural area, embracing a lifestyle not too different from the people they wanted to serve. Gandhi pursued the ideal of village service. For him service was fundamental to community upliftment.

He did not even use the word 'development' because of its linear nature. In linear development the ideal is to move from a self-sufficient, subsistence, self-sustaining economy to one where the ever-increasing desire for material goods is considered to be a sign of progress. This kind of development implies that rural cultures are backward and urban-industrial societies are advanced. Value judgements are made. Gandhi did not see development as a product of human-imposed industrial design; rather he saw it as an unfolding process of life. Working with the underprivileged was a form of service which was as beneficial to those who served as to those who were served. The word 'development' carries within it a sense of patronage, whereas service embodies an attitude of mutuality and humility. The ideal of service is to find a sense of satisfaction in the service itself rather than in outcomes and targets.

Seva or service is one of the cardinal sattvic principles of Hinduism. From ancient times, sages, saddhus and householders have practised and promoted the ideal of service in every aspect of personal and community life. In homes and temples Hindus must perform certain acts of service for the smooth functioning of society and as a means of self-realisation. Hindu temples used to be, and to a lesser extent still are, networks for the provision of food, employment, housing and psychological support as an expression of the service principle.

Mahatma Gandhi renewed the tradition of service and gave it new meaning. He urged people to offer service to others irrespective of religious affiliation, caste or class distinctions. His companions included people from different religious backgrounds such as Christians, Muslims, Buddhists, Sikhs and Jains. Together they followed the path of service to end injustice, oppression, exploitation, deprivation and social divisions. For Gandhi, service became a revolutionary principle not only to free India from colonial rule but also to build it as a society based on compassion and respect on the one hand, and security of livelihood on the other, so that diversity of cultures, religions and ethnicities could flourish and deprivation would be brought to an end.

Gandhi, the champion of the *Seva* concept, held no office, pursued no career, accumulated no wealth and desired no fame. Yet millions of people in India and around the world are still captivated by his life and his achievements. He inspired so many because he practised what he preached, he lived the change he wanted to see in the world, and his message was none other than his life itself. He was an honest seeker of truth, a fearless defender of the weak and an uncompromising practitioner of non-violence.

The Gandhian idea of service is an example of sattvic development *par excellence*. In order to understand his approach, let me give you a brief summary of his background. He was born as Mohandas Karamchand Gandhi on 2 October 1869 in the town of Porbandar in Gujarat in western India. His father, a devout Hindu, was Prime Minister in his native princely state, his mother was a Jain. The young Gandhi was sent to England to study law. Then he went to South Africa to practise it. There he was thrown out of a segregated train on the ground of his colour. Shaken by this unjust encounter, Gandhi mounted a non-violent civil disobedience campaign to expose the evils of Apartheid. Inspired by the writings and example of Henry David Thoreau, he stirred the political circles of South Africa. He called his campaign Truth Force, in Sanskrit *Satyagraha*. Faced with the brute force of weapons and prisons, Gandhi used the power of non-violence and truth and proved its superiority. Surprised by the use of this technique, the perpetrators of Apartheid found themselves confused and powerless.

On returning to India, Gandhi refined his techniques of *Satyagraha* and introduced them to empower the people of India to wage their struggle for freedom. His movement became so powerful and effective that even the seemingly all-powerful British Empire could not withstand it, and eventually agreed to grant independence to India. While the freedom struggle was in progress, Gandhi was working on ideas for a new social order for post-colonial India. He believed that there would be no point in getting rid of the British without getting rid of the centralised, exploitative and violent system of governance and the economics of greed that they pursued. Gandhi designed a new trinity to achieve his vision of a new non-violent social order. He called it *Sarvodaya, Swaraj* and *Swadeshi*.

The first of this trinity was *Sarvodaya*, 'the upliftment of all'. 'All rise'—not a few, as in capitalism, not even the greatest good of the greatest number, as in socialism, but each and every one should be taken care of. That is Sarvodaya. The Western system of governance is based on the rule of the majority and is called democracy. This was not good enough for Gandhi. He wanted no division between the majority and the minority. He wanted to serve the interests of all. Democracy is also limited to care for the interests of human beings. Democracy working with capitalism favours the few who have capital. Democracy with socialism favours the majority, but is still limited to humans. Sarvodaya includes the care of the Earth—of animals, forests, rivers and land. Gandhi's vision is better encapsulated in the concept of *biocracy* rather than democracy.

The second aspect of the Gandhian trinity is *Swaraj*, 'self-government'. Swaraj works to bring about a social transformation through small-scale, decentralised, self-organised and self-directed participatory structures of governance. It also implies self-transformation, self-discipline and self-restraint. Thus Swaraj is a moral, ethical, ecological and spiritual concept and therefore a sattvic method of governance.

The third part of the trinity is *Swadeshi*, 'local economy'. Gandhi opposed mass production, favouring production by the masses. Work for him was as much a spiritual necessity as an economic one. So he insisted on the principle that every member of society should be engaged in manual work. Manufacturing in small workshops and adherence to arts and crafts feeds the body as well as the soul, he said. He believed that long-distance transportation of goods, competitive trading and relentless economic growth are rajasic, verging towards tamasic, because they destroy the fabric of human communities. Within the context of *Sarvodaya*, *Swaraj* and *Swadeshi*, taking care of each other and caring for the Earth, constantly and regularly, development emerges through *seva* and is sattvic development.

The English translation of *seva* as service does not convey the depth of its meaning. For example, one can be paid for a service but seva is offered as a gift. Seva implies devotion and a long-term commitment. It is good in itself, irrespective of results, outcomes and achievements. The person performing seva does not try to change the world but to serve the world. When one wishes to change others, there is a certain amount of rajasic hubris involved. When we want to change the world, we know what is good for the world and we want to shape it to our image and to our ends.

The person engaged in serving the world accepts his or her limitations and offers himself or herself for the wellbeing of the other, believing that the other is none other than I, and I am none other than the other. There is no duality, nor separation between the one serving and the one served. Both exist in a web of relationships and both are seeking spiritual fulfilment as well as material and physical wellbeing. It was this spirit which inspired many thousands of Gandhian workers to commit themselves to sattvic development through service.

Gandhi himself established an ashram in central India close to the city of Wardha and called it *Seva Gram*, 'village of service'. There he practised a life of prayer, meditation and study of the sacred texts of all religions. Also from there he worked for the eradication of untouchability, care for the sick including lepers, women's emancipation, village sanitation, organic agriculture, and educating people in spinning, weaving and other arts and crafts.

In the Gandhian view the poor are poor not because they are unskilled or uneducated or stupid or lazy. They are poor because the rich and powerful have unjustly deprived them of access to land, materials, tools and other sources of livelihood. Therefore, the sharing of the sources of livelihood with everyone in the community was the first step towards sattvic development. The problem, as Gandhi saw it, was not poverty; the problem was affluence and injustice. It was not the poor who needed developing; it was the rich who needed to learn to share. For Gandhi, God is in the poor; and He even comes to your door in the form of a beggar. Giving and sharing is a spiritual practice rather than an act of pride and condescension. It is the greed of the affluent which is the cause of poverty. Meeting the material needs of everyone enables society as a whole to pursue the path of sattvic development. And it is in the sattvic sphere where the greatest human fulfilment and happiness lie. Through service, the work of development is transformed into a sattvic practice.

The aim of development underpinned by sattvic values is to seek quality of life and to create a life of elegant simplicity rather than a high standard of living. 'Live simply so that others may simply live' is the motto of those who follow the Gandhian approach. Gandhi promoted the idea of development as service and service as development.

Vinoba Bhave and his Vision of Sattvic Development as Sharing

FOLLOWING MAHATMA GANDHI there have been two significant movements in the Indian subcontinent which have exemplified development as a sattvic undertaking. The first was led by Vinoba Bhave, a close associate of Gandhi, and the second by A. T. Ariyaratne of Sri Lanka.

Vinoba Bhave urged landowners all over India to give one-sixth of their land to the landless as an act of sharing. He walked over 100,000 miles, the length and breadth of India, speaking to landowners in villages and towns, arousing their compassion and awareness. His message was simply that individual and family wellbeing lay in the wellbeing of the community and society as a whole. Such wellbeing can only be achieved by sharing.

Such was the landowners' response to Vinoba's appeal that four million acres of land were donated and transferred to the landless. This was far more than the Indian government achieved with its attempt at redistribution of land under the Land Ceiling Act. Vinoba believed that once the poor had land and their local economy was protected, they would be able to earn their livelihood through a combination of craft, crops and cultural activities. This was an example of development as sharing and sharing as development. Vinoba believed that development emerging out of sharing is sattvic development.

He used to say that since we do not own the air, water and sunshine, how can we own the land? The land was here before we came into this world and it will remain after we have gone from this world. The land will feed, nourish and sustain life generation after generation. We are transient beings, trustees for a while before we pass on the care of the land to the next generation. His campaign was for a change of system, from ownership to trusteeship. He initiated a land revolution as a key to sattvic development.

Secular development is often aimed at creating an economy which will provide jobs and generate money. It is commonly believed that money is wealth. Vinoba challenged this view. He believed that a sense of sharing, a sense of community, a sense of belonging, as well as clean air, unpolluted water, access to land, and the skills to make things and grow food are true wealth. Money is not wealth. It is a mere means of exchange. Money may have a place in our lives, but it must be kept in its place and never be confused with wealth or treated as a source of power. With such a sattvic philosophy he was able to bring about a change of heart in landowner and landless alike. By distributing land he was not distributing ownership; rather he was creating a system of trusteeship. Many thousands of villages brought their entire landholdings under trusteeship; private ownership was abolished and gifts of land are held in trust by the community.

Vinoba inspired well-educated city dwellers to go and live in poor villages and become fully resident there. They were required to build their own dwellings from local materials and live like the locals. There should be no distinction between providers and recipients of development. It is only by identifying with the poor and sharing their pain and problems deeply that those who work with the poor can fully participate in the process of change and transformation from within.

Vinoba also encouraged and inspired village people themselves to become catalysts of change, so that workers from outside and workers from within the village communities engaged together in planning and organising the activities needed for reconstruction. The ideas of development were not to be imported and imposed on the local population: the process of change must grow from within.

The work included the organisation of basic education. This involved the teaching of spinning, weaving and crafts; singing, dancing and festivals; religious values of sharing, caring and compassion; knowledge of crops, water conservation and reforestation; traditional methods of health-care and disease prevention through herbs and nutrition. Education in this case was not a route to a certificate for a job in town but a way of enabling people to take care of themselves, their communities and their environment. This education was not only for children but for people of all ages. It was a method of learning by making and doing. It was a process of participating in the exchange of information. Idealism prevailed. No one was paid a salary; everyone involved grew their food and shared whatever was available.

This was all in stark contrast to the government's rajasic development programmes, where officials were paid high salaries, came in suits in their cars and had ready-made answers for every problem! And of course it was just the opposite of tamasic development where land was grabbed by the rich to build big dams, car factories or so-called Special Economic Zones, such as exist in modern India and China.

Vinoba Bhave's movement was an example of sattvic development *par excellence.*

Ariyaratne and his Vision of Sattvic Development as Friendship

THE SECOND MOVEMENT inspired by Gandhi was *Sarvodaya* in Sri Lanka, initiated by a Buddhist teacher, A. T. Ariyaratne. The word, as stated earlier, was originally coined by Mahatma Gandhi and means a way of thinking, living and acting which is beneficial not only to humans but to all other creatures as well. It has been translated as the upliftment of all. The word at once implies ecological, spiritual and social development. It conveys the idea of development as the self-realisation of humans, animals, plants and every other form of life. It is a most inclusive concept.

When Ariyaratne was a university professor in Colombo he started taking some of his students to villages during weekends and holidays. They offered their services for the restoration of communities. Being a Buddhist, Ariyaratne believed that friendship was the most altruistic and selfless form of relationship. All other relationships, such as those between parents and children, husbands and wives, workers and managers, teachers and disciples, imply certain expectations. But friendship involves unconditional acceptance of the other. Ariyaratne and his students gave their time, talent and skill as an unconditional gift. They declared themselves to be friends of the people and friends of the Earth. The word for friendship in Buddhism is *metta*, and one of the names of Gautama the Buddha is Maitreya. He is not a guru, a master, a prophet, or a divine being, he is simply a friend—*Maitreya.*

Ariyaratne's message of development has spread far and wide in Sri Lanka. Many thousands of rural poor have begun to help each other in the spirit of friendship; spirituality and development have truly come together. Self-help as well as mutual help, self-reliance as well as interdependence are the key concepts of this movement. Aid from outside agencies is minimal, merely the icing on the cake. The real cake is made of the local economy, local resources, local people and local talent. This is a shining example of sattvic development inspired by the concept of engaged Buddhism.

The Buddha's teachings are not merely intellectual, nor are they confined to the scriptures for academic study and debate in monasteries and temples. The Buddha's teachings have to be practised in everyday life. If Buddhism becomes disengaged from the world and does not address the sufferings, problems and preoccupations of daily life, then that is irrelevant Buddhism.

Spirituality without social engagement is reduced to a self-centred practice, leading to a dead end. Social engagement without spirituality, on the other hand, becomes the pursuit of power and self-aggrandisement. Therefore, the idea of engaged Buddhism integrates spirituality and society, enhancing both, thus working to bring an end to economic as well as psychological suffering and liberating humanity from physical hunger as well as psychological cravings. Dr Ariyaratne has made spirituality relevant to development by promoting friendship as development and development as friendship.

Radical Christian Views of Development as Liberation

ALTHOUGH THE WORD 'SATTVIC' is rooted in the Indian philosophy, sattvic motivations can be found in many traditions. Liberation theologians are examples of that. Development resulting from friendship is truly sattvic development. There has been a long tradition of Christian missionaries running schools and hospitals in poverty-stricken areas. The education and medicine they provide are often offered with mixed motives. Those who benefit are expected to convert to the religion of the missionaries. The native, tribal and indigenous religions are considered inferior. Thus the purity and sanctity of the spiritual attitude is corrupted by organised and institutionalised religions whose missionaries take their guidance from far away, importing rituals and rules from foreign lands or alien cultures. Although there are economic benefits to the local population, such bartering of religion for goods and services causes resentment and resistance. Moreover, this kind of charity never challenges the unjust, inequitable social order which causes the poverty in the first place. Development brought about by missionaries reinforces the status quo. Because of such mixed motives, missionary development falls within the category of rajasic development.

However, a number of radical Catholic priests in Central and South America are leading a movement of Liberation Theology. For them a religion is no religion if it perpetuates oppression and ignores the subjugation of the weak. If the Church sides with the rajasic forces of the state, the landowners, the industrialists, the multinational corporations and big business rather than with the downtrodden, then it becomes part of the problem rather than part of the solution. Talk of democracy, human rights, the rule of law, the free market, a free press and similar grand concepts rings hollow when social and political relationships derive their authority from a basically unjust and exploitative social order. The responsibility of religious people in such situations is not to conspire and collude with vested interests but to stand up and arouse the people to work for non-violent change. In Liberation Theology solidarity with the oppressed becomes a religious practice.

A primary tool of Liberation Theology is to make people conscious of their condition and their power to change it. The oppressive system can only operate with the co-operation of the oppressed, and the oppressed co-operate with the oppressor because they are unaware of their rights and their power. Through political education people rise up against the causes of their poverty and deprivation and recognise development as liberation and liberation as development.

There have been many thinkers and activists promoting Liberation

Theology. Leonardo Boff is one of them. A member of a Christian community in Brazil, he has preached an activist gospel for decades. In 2001 he was awarded the Right Livelihood Award for his outspoken critique of consumerist culture, which damages the life of the people and of the planet. His overwhelming concern is: how can we propound the love and mercy of God to the millions who starve?

Boff is working to liberate oppressed poor, oppressed blacks, oppressed native peoples, oppressed women, and also the Earth, which is oppressed by human greed. He believes that religious faith must express itself in political action and social mobilisation in order to bring about justice and dignity for the unjustly humiliated.

Inspired by the work of Leonardo Boff and other Liberation Theologians, many church communities throughout Latin America, even in the face of the displeasure of the Vatican, have organised campaigns of mass awareness in order to respond to the plight of the poor and oppressed. Now the call of Liberation Theology is ringing the bells of conscience in Africa, in Asia and even in Europe and the USA. Many churches are moving out of their missionary mode and embracing the cause of liberation as a prerequisite to development.

Even though Liberation Theologians may never have heard of the term 'sattvic development', my experience of these radical Christians leads me happily to apply the term to their movement. Liberation Theology stems from profoundly sattvic aspirations.

A Scientific Vision of Development as Homage to Gaia

AS IT IS DARING to put the idea of sattva within the context of Christian theology, it is even more problematic to put it and science together. But in my view Gaia and sattva are completely compatible. When we speak of development, the first thought is the economic development of the people. It is an anthropocentric concept. The work carried out by governmental and non-governmental agencies is at best addressed to the human rights of the downtrodden and to alleviating the conditions of hunger, ill health and illiteracy of the poor. But James Lovelock, a scientist, speaks for the rights of micro- and macro-organisms. He stands up for the bacteria and the butterflies. In his view, rivers have rights to flow and remain unpolluted, rocks have rights to stand where they are, and forests have rights to be free of the chainsaw and human intervention. For Lovelock, the Earth acts as if it were a living organism, maintaining its life forms, its climate, its seasons and weather patterns as a self-sustaining, self-governing, self-organising and self-correcting system.

According to Gaia Theory combined with Deep Ecology, as presented by Stephan Harding in his book *Animate Earth,* human life is intrinsically no more and no less significant than other forms of life. In the Gaian worldview, the idea that humans are the superior species having dominion or stewardship over the Earth and therefore that human development takes precedence over the rights of the Earth is preposterous. Gaia Theory goes beyond utilitarian environmentalism. It challenges the view that the natural world is there to be managed as a resource for human use.

Rather than worshipping a God outside the universe as a creator, Gaia Theory suggests that the appropriate attitude is reverence for the Earth itself. Through such reverential ecology it is recognised that humans and other forms of life evolve together and live symbiotically in deep dependence on each other and on the Earth. Each form of existence, animate and inanimate, has intrinsic value: they are bound together in kinship. Here Gaian science and the sattvic worldview of India meet: the whole Earth is one family.

By naming the theory 'Gaia' after the Greek goddess of the Earth (*geo* as in geology and geography) we are invited to revere the Earth. Thus development arising out of a Gaian worldview naturally takes on sattvic dimensions. The attitude of reverence becomes the bridge between science and sattva. Thus development is homage to Gaia, and respecting Gaia is true development. Economic development at the expense of the ecosystems of Gaia falls into the rajasic or tamasic arena. Gaian development embraces the whole natural world rather than just the human species. It puts an obligation on the seekers of human development to include restraint and limits on consumption. It questions the goal of unlimited economic growth and human dependence on fossil fuels and mass production, which cause global warming and climate change.

In my view, Gaian development is intrinsically sattvic. Human development without damaging the fragile fabric of Gaia can only take place if we maintain a sattvic way of life. So if we adopt the simple and sattvic quality of life, then we should be able to share the gifts of Gaia and live happily together without destroying her. Human development is sustainable only within the limits of the finite Earth.

Liberation

Practise non-violence; do no harm.
Practise plurality; there are many truths.
Possess nothing; there is abundance.

—

The liberated is not long or short,
Large or small, circular or square,
Black or white, male or female;
The liberated is beyond form and beyond conditions,
Beyond this and that;
All just is all, and all is unlimited.

Mahavir

Chapter Six

SATTVIC PRINCIPLES IN JAIN TRADITION

Equality of Species

IF I CAN STRETCH the idea of the three *gunas* to certain Christian and scientific movements, then applying that idea to the Jain tradition presents no problem. There has been much interaction between the Ayurvedic tradition and the Jains. Non-violence to animals as well as to humans is one of the fundamental principles of the Jains. For them, to be sattvic is to be non-violent.

Over 2,000 years ago Jains calculated that there were 8.4 million living species upon the Earth. This amazingly long list included eagles, swans, whales, tigers, elephants, snakes, worms, bacteria, fungi, air, water, fire, rocks, and everything which is natural and alive. Jains could be called animists — for them, everything natural is living, and all life is sacred. Any kind of harm to any form of life is to be avoided or minimised. Of course, the survival of one form of life depends upon the sacrifice of another, therefore it is not possible to be completely non-violent, yet Jains are required to limit the taking of life even for survival. I am sure Gaian scientists such as James Lovelock and Stephan Harding would be very comfortable among Jains.

Human beings are only one of those 8.4 million species. They have no more rights than any other species. All living beings, human and other than human, have an equal right to life. Not only do humans have no absolute right to take, to control, or to subjugate other forms of life, but they also have extra obligations to practise non-violence, and to be humble in the face of the mysterious, glorious, abundant and extraordinary phenomena of the living world. This ecological humility is basically the most essential sattvic quality of the Jains.

One story best expresses the Jain attitude toward animals.

Once Parshwanath, a young prince, arriving as a bridegroom, with his marriage entourage, at the house of his bride, saw near the house an enclosure of animals, tightly packed, waiting to be slaughtered. Shocked by the cry of the animals, the prince enquired, "Why are those animals being kept in such cruel conditions?" His aides replied, "They are for the feast of the wedding party."

The young prince was overwhelmed with compassion. Arriving at the wedding chamber, he spoke with the father of the princess. "Immediately and unconditionally all those animals enclosed to be slaughtered for the marriage feast must be freed," he said. "Why?" responded the father. "The animals are there for the pleasure of humans. Animals are our slaves and our meat. How can there be any feast without their flesh?!"

Prince Parshwanath could not believe what he had just heard. He exclaimed, "Animals have souls, they have consciousness, they are our kith and kin, they are our ancestors. They wish to live as much as we do; they have feelings and emotions. They have love and passion; they fear death as much as we do. Their instinct for life is no less than ours. Their right to live is as fundamental as our own. I cannot marry, I cannot love and I cannot enjoy life if animals are enslaved and killed." Without further ado he rejected the plans for his marriage. He even discarded the comfortable life of a prince, and he responded to his inner calling to go out and awaken the sleepy masses who had been conditioned to kill animals. He led the movement for animal compassion.

According to the story, the animal kingdom welcomed Parshwanath as the prophet of the weak and the wild. They gathered around him in response to his calls for kindness. The birds sat upon the tree nearby; fish came to the corner of the lake where Parshwanath meditated. Elephants, lions, foxes, rabbits, rats, insects and ants paid homage to him. One day, finding Parshwanath soaked by the heavy rain of the monsoon, the king of the cobras stood on his tail and created an umbrella with his huge head.

Thousands upon thousands of people in villages, towns and cities were moved by the teachings of Parshwanath. They renounced meat and took up the work of animal welfare. The princess whom Parshwanath was to have married was so inspired that she decided to remain unmarried and dedicate herself to the care of animals and all other living beings. Having lost a daughter and would-be son-in-law to the cause of compassion, the king himself underwent transformation. He announced that all animals were to be respected in his kingdom, and that there would be no hunting, no shooting, no caging and no pets.

There are twenty-four Great Liberators in the Jain Lineage. Adinath was the first. Parshwanath was the twenty-third. The twenty-fourth was Mahavir, who lived 2,600 years ago. He revived the Jain religion as it is practised today. All the twenty-four Great Liberators have an animal associated with them, symbolising that in Jain teachings the place of animals is central. Love is not love if it does not include love of animals, birds, plants and all other forms of life. What kind of compassion is it which adores and reveres human life but ignores the slaughter of animals? This is why the Jains consider vegetarian food as the only food which is sattvic and therefore acceptable.

Mahavir was called *Jina*, which means the conqueror of inner enemies such as ego, pride, anger and delusion. Thus followers of *Jina* became 'Jains'.

Mahavir, born as a prince, simply realised that there is more to life than the endless pursuit of rajasic gains such as fame, fortune and power. In fact, fame, fortune and power are the bringers of 'unhappiness'. They create fear and curtail freedom. This notion was not based in any intellectual theories; rather it was based on his experience. He left the kingdom for the forest in search of wisdom, liberation and enlightenment. After a long life of meditation and contemplation, he came to the conclusion that everyone needs to practise the seven sattvic rules of life.

1. Non-violence of the Mind, Speech and Action

MAHAVIR SAID THAT non-violence must begin in the mind. Unless the mind is filled with compassion, non-violence is not possible. Unless one is at ease in the inner world, one cannot practise non-violence in the external world. If the tongue speaks sweet words to other people yet the mind is condemning them, then that is not non-violence. The seeds of non-violence have to be sown in the mind. Keeping the mind pure is therefore an essential part of non-violence. A pure mind means a consciousness that is uncorrupted, uncontaminated and undiluted with the desire to control others.

We are violent because we wish to control others. Those who eat meat think that 'animals and fish are there for our food'—everything is for us and we are the masters of nature. This is the violence of the mind, which leads to physical violence.

Mahavir saw the world as a sacred place. The birds, the flowers, the butterflies and the trees are sacred; rivers, soil and oceans are sacred. Life as a whole is sacred. All our interactions with other people and with the natural world must be based on this sacred trust, on deep reverence for all life.

Non-violence of the mind should be translated into non-violence of speech. Harmful, harsh, untrue, unnecessary, unpleasant and offensive speech is violence. Skilful use of language is a necessary art in the pursuit of non-violent communication. Mahavir insisted that we must understand others fully before we speak. Language can express only a partial truth; therefore non-violence is an essential guide to our spoken words. 'Speak the truth, but speak it sweetly; if you cannot speak it sweetly, then keep silent while you learn the art of skilful speech.' Non-violence is a higher principle than the truth. We may not know what the truth is; today's truth may not be tomorrow's truth. Practise non-violence of speech while you speak the truth. The Jains celebrate diversity of thoughts and truths, but they insist on the common ground of non-violence.

Non-violence of mind and speech leads to non-violence of action. Ends cannot justify means; means must be compatible with ends. Therefore, all human actions must be friendly, compassionate and non-aggressive. Do no harm—no ifs and buts, no compromise. Mahavir's non-violence is unconditional caring and kindness to all beings.

Thus non-violence is the paramount principle of the Jains. All other principles stem from non-violence. Non-violence is first and last. Because all life is sacred we may not violate or take advantage of those life forms which may be weaker than ourselves. *Ahimsa* is much more than 'Live and let live', it is 'Live and love!'

I began this book with the problem of anguish in our age. Throughout I have made the point that the cause of this anguish is clear: we adopt bad means to achieve good ends. We cannot bring an end to anguish as long as there is no congruence between the means and the ends. Much of our civilisation follows the means of violence—be it overt or covert violence. The reality is that ours is a violent civilisation. Industrialisation, centralisation, urbanisation, globalisation, materialism, capitalism and consumerism have all inflicted a great deal of violence on individuals, communities and nature. This violence has now culminated in violence to the climate; we are facing catastrophic climate change. Violence to people, to animals, to the Earth and to the climate is a continuum. Violence is perhaps the most vile tamasic tendency there is.

The world spends $1,000 billion annually on armies and armaments. Leaders of civilised nations take pride in the possession of nuclear and other weapons of mass destruction. They believe that war will bring peace. In other words, they hope that tamas will lead to sattva. It is like hoping to produce butter by churning sand.

Physical violence is only the outer manifestation of a deep-rooted tamasic streak within the human heart and mind. The desire to conquer and control other people, other nations, and the Earth itself is violence. Such inner desires lead to outer expressions of violence against ourselves, against other cultures and religions, and against life itself.

We poison the Earth with chemicals, fertilisers, pesticides, herbicides and other toxic concoctions to satisfy our greed and try to gain control over the process of natural cycles. We inflict needless cruelty on animals in our factory farms. Factory farming and industrial agriculture are violence.

We annihilate the rainforest, woodlands and hedgerows to create large-scale monoculture commercial farms to grow cash crops so that our immense appetite for market control can be gratified. We sweep the oceans with our fishing nets and destroy fish stocks through massive fishing fleets in order to obtain excessive profits. This is an act of violence to the land and the oceans. We need to practise natural, organic, sattvic farming.

We create the means of mass production, forcing creative human beings to stand by a conveyor belt acting as machines themselves, thus causing the destruction of the human imagination, craftsmanship and artisan production, and a loss of livelihood. Such violent methods of manufacture promote sweatshops, child labour, deprivation and ill health which lead to the breakdown of the social fabric and to increasing poverty. Poverty is violence. We need to work hard to eliminate chronic, tamasic, poverty through the sattvic qualities of caring and sharing.

Factories of mass production generate effluents which pollute the sacred water of rivers, streams and oceans. Smoke from the chimneys causes acid rain, which creates climate change. Pollution is violence. We need to minimise pollution.

Billions of barrels of petroleum are burned to sustain our civilisation. Food, clothing, housing, heating, transportation and every other activity have become dependent on fossil fuel. Excessive carbon emissions cause global warming and enormous amounts of waste. Waste is violence. We need to reduce waste.

We have been violent to the climate, so now the climate is being violent to us; we reap what we sow. Nature acts reciprocally. Our violence to the climate is only the tip of the inbuilt violent tendencies of our civilisation.

Institutionalised and structural violence is as fatal as physical violence. In order to maintain themselves in power, governments institutionalise violence, wage wars and engage in torture, imprisonment and abuse. Such a way of life can hardly be called civilised.

This tamasic culture of violence must be replaced with a sattvic culture of non-violence if we are to sustain life on Earth. This has been the message of many wise teachers, both in the past and in our own time. 'Do no harm' has been the motto of all spiritual traditions. Prophets and visionaries have laid the sattvic path of non-violence before us, but we have chosen to ignore it and follow the tamasic path of violence. The political leaders of the so-called civilised world have turned a blind eye. Instead we have built nuclear weapons and created economies of war. Now we are facing the repercussions of our indifference to the teachings of non-violence and spiritual values. Impending climate chaos and increased insecurity are the natural consequences of our violent way of life. Civilisation without spirituality is a total failure. We have money but lack meaning. We live in an age of anguish; humanity is denuded of human spirit.

There may still be time to change course and recognise the folly of using violent means to achieve the goals of freedom, democracy and human rights. There may still be time to create a culture of non-violence in which a small, simple and elegant way of life can be in balance, harmony and peace with the whole universe. We have to seize the time and realise that the universe is holy, life is sacred, we should harm nothing.

There is no way to peace. Peace *is* the way, said Mahatma Gandhi. This book is an attempt to remind ourselves that there is a peaceful way, and that way is the way of cultivating the human spirit. We are as much human spirit as we are human body, human mind and human intellect. Let us strive to unite the whole of humanity to meet the challenge of global warming through spiritual and non-violent means. Humanity is crying out for spiritual nourishment. The hunger of the human soul can only be satisfied with the food of the spirit, and the human spirit resides in the house of non-violence. Non-violence is the supreme spiritual principle. Non-violence is the foremost sattvic quality. Put non-violence first, and the rest will follow.

Economics, technology and science alone cannot provide the answers; as Albert Einstein said, we cannot solve a problem with the same mindset and same values that caused the problem in the first place. He was right. Global warming has been caused by the blind application of technology, science, and economics, with the motivation of greed, profit and power. To find the true answer to the crisis of global warming we must follow a different path, the path of the spirit, of elegant simplicity, of less and local, of natural, healthy and wholesome living, the path of making rather than consuming, participating rather than controlling, and caring rather than wasting; the path of sattvic rather than tamasic qualities.

Sustainable living and a stable climate are a spiritual imperative.

2. Living Within the Limits

THE SECOND RULE IS *Sanyama,* a Jain word for sattvic. Sanyama means 'simplicity', 'self-restraint', 'sufficiency', 'frugality'. We need to learn to be satisfied with less. The idea that whatever we have, or however much we have, is never enough, is the source of anguish. Therefore we are required to move from 'more and more' to 'enough and sufficient'.

For Jains there is nothing lacking in the world; there is just the abundance of Nature. Only when we want to own, control and possess it, do we create scarcity. We can never possess everything, but we always want more. This possessiveness is the source of scarcity. The moment we are satisfied, and do not want to control and possess, we have abundance. Paradoxically this abundance is only available to those who can learn to live within the limits of their needs.

The principle of restraint is very relevant in our modern world. We are encouraged to buy, to shop, to possess and to expand our material wealth incessantly. We think, we live and work as if there are no limits. The dominant ideology of our time is to conquer and control nature and constantly add to and accumulate material possessions.

Such consumerism has created confusion between need and greed. The Jain response to this confusion is that we should not only overcome our greed, but even reduce what we consider to be our need. Cars, washing machines, dishwashers, televisions, DVD and CD players, iPods, mobile phones, computers and other gadgets have come to be considered as 'basic needs'. But a great deal of time is spent on doing monotonous, unpleasant and soul-destroying work to acquire these gadgets, and when they have been acquired even more time is spent in using, repairing, maintaining and replacing them. They quickly become obsolete, so we have to work hard to keep acquiring up-to-date models. Often, the equipment sits in attics gathering dust. Garages and garden sheds are filled with unused items, and yet we go on acquiring more and more.

It is not that people are naturally greedy and acquisitive. The media and the advertising industry constantly work to cajole, persuade, entice and pressurise people into buying what they neither require nor desire. Governments also demand that their citizens consume at an ever-increasing rate in order to keep the economy going and people employed. Consumerism has become a patriotic duty. Because people are so busy with the business of consumerism there is little time left to make, to create, to sing, to dance, to enjoy, to celebrate and to be, no time for the family, friends, or neighbours.

In this age of materialism we are persuaded to live under the rajasic reign of quantity. The Jains believe in the sattvic reign of quality. They ask themselves three questions before acquiring new possessions:

Do I need it? Can I live without it? If I have lived without it for so long, why can I not live without it in the future?

Are the things that I am acquiring durable? Are they made to last? And, are they made using environmentally friendly methods and materials?

Are these things beautiful? Are they well made, life-enhancing and aesthetically pleasing?

These may be uncomfortable questions in a world which is ruled by the ideology of economic growth. Government, media, industry, commerce, business, education, culture and even religions measure their success and failure in terms of their economic performance.

International organisations have been established to foster unlimited and unchecked economic growth. The World Trade Organisation, The World Bank, the International Monetary Fund and the European Union are some of the more familiar world bodies asserting their powerful influence to promote economic growth. Multinational corporations exercise much greater power and influence than governments in turning citizens into consumers. In fact some of those corporations are richer than many nations. The annual turnover of companies such as Mitsubishi, General Motors, Ford, Shell and Toyota are greater than that of countries like Indonesia, Thailand, Turkey, Malaysia and Iran, so the power of these rajasic corporations is immense in conditioning our minds to consume, consume and consume.

Without knowing it, we are truly living under the dictatorship of the dollar, the euro and the pound. This dictatorship is more dangerous because it is subtle and masked behind the lofty aim of increasing human wellbeing and improving living standards. But in reality this kind of unrestrained pursuit of possessions is bringing a catastrophic situation in terms of environmental sustainability, social justice, economic equity and climate stability.

In this context the sattvic idea of restraint, traditionally practised by millions of Jains for more than 2,000 years, is extremely potent. Mahavir said, “Even the angels bow to those who practise restraint.” He set a supreme example himself. Being the son of a king, he found that all his time was taken in the management of material possessions. The palaces, the furniture, the hundreds of horses, the elephants and domestic animals, the thousands of acres of land, the hundreds of servants and all the other paraphernalia such as robes, jewellery, shoes, thrones etc. were absorbing all his attention, and he had no space left to attend to the needs of his soul. And so he decided to leave his kingdom. He showed that to be happy you need very little.

Mahavir taught us to be alert, aware and conscious of the amount of material possessions we accumulate and use. For example, every morning after meditation, practising Jains put a limit on the number of items they are going to eat or wear, the distance they will travel, and the things they are going to purchase. Their aim is to reduce their consumption from the previous day, and find satisfaction in using a few things well rather than many things carelessly. This is not to say that one has to be extreme and give up everything; the intention is to appreciate the importance of frugality and give proper value and care to the things upon which we depend, rather than being wasteful. The point is not to become obsessed with the limits one has set oneself, and suffer guilt if the aim is not achieved; the true meaning of restraint is to be mindful of our relationship with the material world, and to create a better balance between material needs and spiritual needs.

3. Austerity

THE THIRD RULE IS *Tapas* (literally 'heat'), or self-purification. This is one of the most significant contributions of Jain spirituality. As humans purify their physical bodies, so they also need to purify their inner soul. As we burn old, unwanted and spoilt possessions, so we also need to burn the burdens of our mind. The mind becomes polluted with harmful thoughts. The consciousness becomes contaminated by ego, greed, pride, anger and fear. Souls suffer because of desires, attachments and anguish. So Mahavir devised ways to purify the mind, the soul and the consciousness by burning inner impurities; he called this *Tapas*.

Fasting, meditation, restraint, rest, pilgrimage and service to others fall within the ways of sattvic austerity.

4. Truth

TRUTH MEANS UNDERSTANDING and realising the true nature of existence and the true nature of oneself. It means accepting reality as it is and being truthful to it, seeing things as they are. Truth means 'Do not lie' in its deepest sense: do not have illusions about the world or about yourself. Face the truth without fear. Things are as they are. A person of truth goes beyond mental constructs and realises existence as it is. Living in truth means that we avoid manipulating people or nature. There is no one single truth that any mind can grasp or tongue can express. Being truthful involves being humble and open to new discoveries, and yet accepting that there is no one final or ultimate discovery. Truth is what is: we accept what is as it is; speak of it as it is, and live it as it is. Any individual or group claiming to know the whole truth is by definition engaged in falsehood. Ultimately, life is a great mystery, and we have to accept the truth of that mystery!

5. Non-stealing

NON-STEALING IS AN extension of simplicity and restraint, and means refraining from acquiring goods or services beyond one's essential needs. The Jain understanding of stealing goes further than any legal definition. If we take more from nature than meets our essential need, we are stealing from nature. For example, clearing an entire forest would be seen as a violation of nature's rights and as theft. Similarly, taking from society in the form of housing, food and clothing in excess of one's essential requirements means depriving other people and is therefore theft. If we are using up finite resources at a greater rate than they can be replenished, then we are stealing from future generations. The Jains would give first and then take. Taking before giving is stealing.

6. Safe sex

SAFE SEX MEANS RESTRAINED sexual conduct. It is love without lust. It means fidelity in marriage or long, committed relationships. Any thoughts, speech or acts that demean, debase or abuse the body or physical relationship are against the principle of safe sex. The body is the temple of love, and therefore no activity should be undertaken which would defile it.

7. Non-possessiveness

NON-POSSESSIVENESS is an even further extension of simplicity. It means non-accumulation of material things. If no one hoards, owns, possesses or accumulates anything, then no one will be deprived. Non-possessiveness means sharing and living without ostentation and without a display of wealth. Dress, food and furnishings should be simple, elegant, but minimal. 'Simple in means, rich in ends' is the Jain motto.

Unnecessary possessions are a burden, a bondage. Not to acquire what is not necessary is common sense, but such common sense is no longer common. Free yourself from non-essential acquisitions and you will be liberated. It is a moral imperative to live simply so that others may simply live.

Paryushan:
A Festival of Introspection and Forgiveness

ONCE EVERY YEAR JAINS around the world take eight days off from their work and put their worldly affairs aside in order to devote their full attention to matters of the soul. Many fast, go on spiritual retreats, go through religious rituals and study the sacred texts.

On 357 days of the year we carry out our responsibilities to our business, our family and our career. Of course, we try to put our principles into practice in everyday life. All ordinary activities are to be performed with the greatest awareness and mindfulness. Jain spirituality is for everyday practice. Nevertheless, the Jains have designated the special period of eight days as a time of reflection, purification and renewal. They call it *Paryushan*.

During the year we might have accumulated mental and emotional clutter in our lives. We might have gathered unnecessary baggage of pride, fear, animosity, greed, ego and delusions in our thoughts and feelings. We might have nursed rajasic desires or even tamasic tendencies. So Paryushan is the time to clear that clutter and make a bonfire of that tamasic junk, that rajasic rubbish which is corrupting our minds, our lives and our relationships.

During the year we may have harmed or offended someone, knowingly or unknowingly. Therefore the greatest challenge of Paryushan is to go through the fire of forgiveness. In Jain tradition forgiveness is a supreme sattvic quality of the soul. All other qualities, such as generosity, humility and compassion are implicit in forgiveness. At the time of Paryushan the Jains proclaim that no dispute, no disagreement, no derision, no quarrel, no fight and no war should be allowed to linger more than one year. Paryushan is the time to heal, to mend, to include, to embrace, to settle disputes and to unite with everyone, without exception.

Forgiveness is the foundation of friendship. Friendship is the house of unconditional love, lasting relationships and profound respect for all living beings, humans and other than humans. In this house of friendship the queen of enduring peace reigns.

On the last day of Paryushan the Jains fast for twenty-four hours. This is the fast for forgiveness. During this fast we chant the prayer of forgiveness: "I forgive those who may have injured me and I beg for forgiveness from all whom knowingly or unknowingly I may have harmed. I declare friendship with all living beings; I have enmity towards no one."

Next morning before breaking the fast, every Jain must go personally to everyone he or she can reach on foot and beg for forgiveness and offer forgiveness to acquaintances, friends, relatives and business contacts. To those who cannot be reached personally, a letter is sent, in which we seek forgiveness.

Particular attention is paid to people with whom there is some outstanding problem or dispute. Unless and until forgiveness has been exchanged the fast cannot be broken. If a small dispute is allowed to grow, it can become a giant destructive force for the whole community. Therefore any rift should be dealt with then and there. A stitch in time saves nine. If we have a small cut on the hand, we must wash it, apply ointment and a bandage; if it is ignored it can become septic and may prevent us from living a healthy normal life. In the same way, if a small misunderstanding has arisen due to careless speech, bad temper or prejudice, it should be cleared up immediately. A small spark of anger can burn the whole house of friendship. So the fire of anger should be extinguished at the earliest possible moment.

We need to develop a way of life which minimises friction between ourselves and others. We need to cultivate an attitude of forgiveness and sensitivity to others and we particularly need to observe the principle of non-violence in thought, word and action. If a negative, callous or insulting thought about others comes into our mind, we need to become aware of it and alarm bells should ring. The seeds of conflict, animosity and war are sown in the minds of individuals. Forgiveness necessitates tolerance and acceptance of many ways of being. It also necessitates non-interference in another person's way of life.

The world is filled with conflicts, and those conflicts are encouraged daily by harmful, injurious and negative language. In the Parliament, in newspapers, on radio and television, rivers of negative language flow every day to no good effect. The leaders of our nations set an example which permeates through society, where scoring points becomes the occupation of life.

When we look around the world we find that disputes linger for decades. There are many countries engulfed in racial, religious or national wars, which seem to have no end. If we were able to bring the principle of Paryushan into the political sphere, then we would set a deadline for peace. Compromise, reconciliation, accommodation to divergent interests and, above all, forgiveness would become the imperative for the peaceful co-existence of all peoples. For Jains, Paryushan is a vitally important festival of forgiveness and friendship, a universal week of peace and reconciliation, a week of returning to a calm and sattvic way of life.

Enough is Enough

Fame or life: which is more desired?
Life or goods: which is greater?
Gain or loss: which is more harmful?
Those who are attached will suffer;
Those who hoard will suffer losses;
Those who know when they have enough
will not be disgraced;

Those who know how to stop will not be harmed;

They will go on forever.

Lao Tzu

AFTERWORD

MY TEACHER, VINOBA BHAVE, used the metaphor of a lantern to make it easy to understand the three gunas. A lantern has a glass exterior which gets filled with black soot inside, and the light is dimmed; that dark soot is tamasic. Dust also falls on the lantern, which further diminishes the light; this is rajasic. With attention and mindfulness, the black soot and the grey dust are removed and one is able to receive the full benefit of the light through the transparent glass; the clean glass is sattvic. Our aim in life should be to develop such a clarity and purity that the clear light of truth can shine through.

ALSO BY SATISH KUMAR

NO DESTINATION

An autobiography

"One of the few life-changing books I have ever read. I wish everyone would read it."—Thomas Moore, author of *Care of the Soul*

"Reading this book, you will have the rare pleasure of meeting a warm and witty, thoroughly genuine man, and one whose inspiration will not fail to move you."
—Kirkpatrick Sale, author of *Rebels Against the Future*

320pp 216 x 138mm ISBN 978 1 870098 89 2 £9.95 paperback

THE BUDDHA AND THE TERRORIST

The Story of Angulimala

"It has a lucid clarity and directness that speaks pointedly and movingly to our times. It should touch every heart that meets it."—Pico Iyer, author of *The Global Soul*

An ancient story which brings a message for our time about the importance of looking for the root causes of violence, and of finding peaceful means to end terror.

96pp 174 x 123mm ISBN 978 1 903998 63 2 £4.95 paperback

ALSO BY SATISH KUMAR

YOU ARE, THEREFORE I AM

A Declaration of Dependence

"The life of this vigorous, wise, compassionate and humble man is an example to all of us about how to make the most of our gifts and create our own opportunities to serve humanity's future."
—Hazel Henderson, author of *Creating Alternative Futures*

"Satish Kumar is, for me, the sage of the deep ecology movement."—Fritjof Capra, author of *The Web of Life*

Tracing his own spiritual journey, Satish Kumar considers the sources of inspiration which formed his understanding of the world as a network of multiple and diverse relationships. The book is in four parts. The first describes his memories of conversations with his mother, his teacher and his Guru, all of whom were deeply religious. The second part recounts his discussions with the Indian sage Vinoba Bhave, J. Krishnamurti, Bertrand Russell, Martin Luther King and E.F. Schumacher. These five great activists and thinkers inspired him to engage with social, ecological and political issues. In the third part Satish narrates his travels in India, which have continued to nourish his mind and reconnect him with his roots. The fourth part brings together his world-view, which is based in relationships and the connections between all things, encapsulated in a fundamental Sanskrit dictum '*So Hum*', well-known in India but not in the West, which can be translated as 'You are, therefore I am'.

192pp 234 x 156mm ISBN 978 1 1903998 18 2 £9.95 paperback

Resurgence

Satish Kumar is Editor of *Resurgence* magazine, described in *The Guardian* as "the spiritual and artistic flagship of the green movement". If you would like a sample copy of a recent issue, please contact:

Jeanette Gill, Rocksea Farmhouse,
St. Mabyn, Bodmin, Cornwall PL30 3BR
Telephone & Fax 01208 841824 www.resurgence.org

He is also Director of Programmes at Schumacher College, an international centre for ecological studies. For the latest course programme, please contact:

The Administrator, Schumacher College
The Old Postern, Dartington, Totnes, Devon TQ9 6EA
Telephone 01803 865934 Fax 01803 866899
www.schumachercollege.org